[**YOUNG GUNS**]

YOUNG GUNS

*The Fearless Entrepreneur's Guide to Chasing Your
Dreams and Breaking Out on Your Own*

Robert Tuchman

AMACOM

AMERICAN MANAGEMENT ASSOCIATION

New York • Atlanta • Brussels • Chicago • Mexico City • San Francisco •
Shanghai • Tokyo • Toronto • Washington, D.C.

This publication is designed to provide accurate and authoritative
information in regard to the subject matter covered. It is sold with the
understanding that the publisher is not engaged in rendering legal,
accounting, or other professional service. If legal advice or other expert
assistance is required, the services of a competent professional person
should be sought.

Library of Congress Cataloging-in-Publication Data

Tuchman, Robert.
    Young guns : the fearless entrepreneur's guide to chasing your dreams
and breaking out on your own / Robert Tuchman.
        p.   cm.
    Includes bibliographical references and index.
    ISBN-10: 0–8144–1070–7
    ISBN-13: 978-0-8144-1070-7
    1. New business enterprises.   2. Success in business.   1. Title.

    HD62.5.T83   2009
    658.1'1—dc22
                                                          2008040994

Printing Hole Number

10   9   8   7   6   5   4   3   2   1

CONTENTS

[YOUNG GUNS]

CHAPTER 1

Why Not Me?

*"*Begin challenging your own assumptions. Your assumptions are your windows on the world. Scrub them off every once in awhile, or the light won't come in.*"*

—**Alan Alda, actor, commentator, and activist**

If you're reading these words, I'm going to assume that you're doing so because the idea of starting your own business from scratch sounds exciting to you—*now*.

That's good. In fact, it's great. No business can thrive without excitement and emotional engagement from the founder of that business. And yet, my job—as someone who started a successful business from nothing, and as someone who has worked with, and interviewed for this book, dozens of people who did exactly the same thing—is to let you know that being excited is not enough. There are plenty of businesses that never achieve their potential, despite incredible initial emotion and strong commitment from the people attempting, in vain, to get them off the ground.

It's easy to be excited *now*. But the kind of excitement you feel right now definitely won't see you through what is to come. When I tell aspiring entrepreneurs this, I usually get a nod of agreement and a stern expression of resolve.

Most of the people who nod at me obediently, though, are under a serious misconception. They think that by saying this I mean that, in addition to showing excitement and emotional engagement in their businesses, they have to master the technical skills they currently lack. What are those skills? Accounting, maybe, if they're not accountants; or advertising and promotion, if they're not familiar with those areas. Or maybe it's hiring and personnel that they perceive as their weak spots.

That's not what I'm getting at.

When I tell people that their initial excitement about starting a business is not enough, what I am saying is that their ability to bounce back tomorrow is much more important than their initial excitement. Resiliency, persistence, stick-to-it-ive-ness, a sense of purpose—whatever you want to call it—is the factor I am talking about: entrepreneurs' unique and certain knowledge that they are embarking on the work of their lives, on their true missions, not just for today but also for tomorrow as well and for the foreseeable tomorrows to come. That quality is what *always* makes the difference between a business that succeeds and a business that fails. You need that resiliency if you are to challenge your own assumptions about what will and won't work in your business, and you definitely need it if you are to challenge anyone else's assumptions as well. You should know here and now that you cannot expect to start a successful business from scratch without that resiliency and persistence.

Why Not Me?

In my experience, there is one, and only one, way to generate that quality of being on a personal mission, a mission that endures no matter what happens to you today. You must get into the habit of asking yourself: *Why not me?*

You must use this question daily, and probably hourly, and you must answer it in the right way if you hope to use the ideas in this book to your advantage. You must use those answers to overcome every fear of failure and every ridicule, every doubt, every adversity that enters your mind. Your own answer to this question will be the single most important factor in your personal campaign—your mission—to start a great business from scratch.

Contrary to what you may have heard or read, successful entrepreneurs are not born with a personal sense of mission. They choose to build that sense of mission into their lives. Successful entrepreneurs know that they operate in a world that's filled with people who have all kinds of skills, dreams, and abilities. They make a conscious decision to assume that they, as individuals, belong at the head of their own personal parade through that world.

They ask, in essence, "Why shouldn't it be me who leads the parade?" And they always come up with an answer that gives them the right—and the duty—to lead that parade.

CHAPTER 2

The Decision

"I didn't want to go back to corporate. I was having fun, being creative, and basically, doing the biggest idea possible without someone telling me no. I was tired of being stuck in endless meetings and having boundaries.**"**

—**Ben Sturner, President and Founder, The Leverage Agency**

It happens to most of us at one time or another. You're out on your own. You've got a job, maybe your first real job. It's exciting at first, and you actually feel you might be on the right path. Then you face your first setback. And you start wondering where you really want to go in your life. Beth Silver, managing director at Doubet Consulting, explains how she handled a life-changing situation:

> I had been helping friends with their various businesses for many years—just for fun. One of my friends needed help with his business; he had set up a co-branded deal with a major telecommunications company, and he was looking for help setting up the new venture. At the time, the company where I was working as VP of marketing was losing its funding. I remember the moment clearly. I went into the CEO's office and asked him if he wanted something from Starbucks. He asked me to close the door and sit down. He told me that he was going to have to let me go right then and there. I walked out of his office with the biggest smile on my face, because I knew exactly what I was going to do next. First I spoke to my [former] staff and told them what had happened. Then I called my dad and told him what was going on. Then I got in touch with my friend to talk about his budget for his new venture. It was time to start my company.

The setback can take any number of forms. Maybe it happens the morning you wake up and you can no longer avoid noticing the fact that you're smarter than your boss. Maybe it happens when you decide, for ethical or moral reasons, that you simply can't work for your employer anymore. Maybe the setback comes that first time you are passed up for a promotion, or that morning when you show up to work and realize that a colleague—someone you feel certain you've outperformed—has just been picked to handle the big account you were working so hard for. Or maybe, like Beth, your company's management simply decided to let you go.

Soon enough, everyone feels the corporate world blues. Sometimes this takes the form of a lack of fulfillment on the job; sometimes it takes the form of market upheavals and financial crises. The good news is that this unhappiness can be the catalyst for change that lifts your life up to a whole new level.

Why Not Me?

Notice that I said that the setback you experience *can* serve as a kind of catalyst. The truth is that it doesn't always do that.

Some people encounter a setback and don't do a thing—they simply keep playing the corporate game. Others, however, will say, "That's it—enough already." And they make a move that changes their lives forever.

I remember when "the setback" happened for me. I was working as a trainee for a stockbroker position at the investment bank Lehman Brothers in New York City. Management had assured all the trainees that if we passed the brokerage exam, they would offer each of us a position as full-time broker—with our own clients—after a few months. Those were very long months. That initial stretch was hard enough for me, because I was a salesperson working underneath people I knew I could equal—or exceed. But I watched what was going on around me at Lehman Brothers, and I quickly realized that, regardless of what I had been promised, management had no intention of promoting any of the trainees up the ladder, no matter how good we were.

That realization made me angry and upset. And as I look back now, I am so, so glad that it made me angry and upset. That's when I started to dream of moving on.

But I wasn't sure *how* to move on. Not yet, at any rate.

Every morning while I had my bagel and coffee, I would read the paper about people who were working in various sports-related businesses: sports reporters, sports agents, sports event promoters. "What a way to earn a living," I thought. These people were doing what they loved—and doing quite well. I wanted to be like them, but I wasn't yet ready to take action on that desire.

I went to work for a competitor of Lehman Brothers, Paine Webber. I soon found out that I was no happier there than I had been at Lehman. I was feeling restless. I wasn't happy. At that point, I started to think seriously that making a living in the world of sports was really what I was supposed to be doing. I *could* be a stockbroker, but I didn't *love* the idea of being a stockbroker and I certainly didn't love the idea of working at or near a subsistence wage for the next decade, chasing the dubious promise of becoming a full-fledged player at Paine Webber.

I made a decision. My working world was going to be connected to the world of professional sports. I didn't know much more than that, but I did know that I had determined what I was going to do. To seal the decision, I asked myself an important question: "Why not me?"

Were the people who actually got to work in the world of sports better than I was, smarter than I was, more energetic than I was? I was pretty sure they weren't. That insight made all the difference in achieving my ultimate success. Because I made the decision—not a wish, or a complaint, or a New Year's resolution, but a *decision*—to make a name for myself in an area that made me happy. Immediately, I obtained something that had been eluding me at Lehman Brothers: an unfair advantage!

Building Something Big

That decision—the decision to change my life and my career path—gave me much more to work with than I realized at the time. It gave me a personal stake in a life built around doing something that I loved doing. And that made all the difference. Suddenly, I was building something for *me*. Something big.

I started learning everything I possibly could about this world I wanted to become part of. I began studying all types of sports marketing companies and public relations opportunities. I landed a job at a company called Sports Profiles, located in Chicago. I had read about Sports Profiles in *Entrepreneur* magazine, and I felt that this was a company involved in sports that I might be able to work for. They sold local sports publications in Los Angeles and Chicago, and they needed an advertising sales rep to work from home in New York City. I took the job with no base salary—100 percent commission.

I soon realized that most of the people who were buying ads from me were asking for "added value"—a term in the advertising world that means tickets, travel packages to events, and other perks that go along with buying an advertisement. Then I suddenly realized that the people I was talking to were more concerned with the added value than they were with the ads! That was one of my "lightbulb moments."

I said to myself, "Here is a business idea that's right for me: why not sell the perks instead of the ads?"

Why Sports Made Sense for Me

Back in college, years before I went to Lehman Brothers, I had thought I would become a sports journalist. I had made it through one of the top sports journalism schools in the country, Boston University. It had been a very competitive program, and that suited me because I was a pretty competitive guy.

After I graduated, though, I got my first view of the journalism career path. I put together a resume and recorded a videotape of me doing a mock report, and I sent my package to hundreds of television stations across the country. Nothing happened.

I ended up taking a weekend job with a company called "Sportsphone," reading scores to people who would call in to find out the scores of games that took place around the country. (Of course, this was before the advent of the Internet.) During the week I worked at Lehman Brothers, just to pay the bills. That's when I started thinking about combining both worlds. What if I could combine my passion for sports with my sales ability? I might be able to build a whole company around selling corporate sports packages.

It was a turning point in my life.

The Decision Comes First

The sports packaging idea carried me toward the business plan that was positively right for *me*. What's right for you? Only you can figure that out. Here's the part that's important: The decision to change your life comes first.

The truth is that I didn't exactly know what I was going to do when I said goodbye to the big brokerage houses. I only knew that what I would be doing would be big—and that it was going to connect me to the world of sports, which I loved. Once I made the decision, I was able to realize how, in the years leading up to that decision, I had been reinforcing two critical habits that would prepare me to carry out my life's work.

1. I was building my knowledge base.

2. I was learning how to change course in a way that made strategic sense, based on what I wanted to accomplish.

These were the two habits that made my company—and my dream—possible. And, believe me when I tell you, both of those habits would be essential for building my company!

Read This Part Twice

Back in college, I had dreamed of interviewing major sports figures, writing books, and spending time at major sporting events—all part of what I did for a living. So when I sent out the hundreds of interview tapes and didn't even get any nibbles, I could have chosen to see that as a failure. Actually, though, that period in my life turned out to be incredibly important and accounted for a major part of the success that followed. Why? Because I was learning the importance of *resilience*.

Years later, what am I doing? As the CEO of a major sports-event consulting firm I have a weekly Internet radio show that's built around my interviews with major sports figures. I'm writing books. And I'm spending my time at major sporting events. That's my job!

Hey, why not you, too?

Who said I had to wait for some guy at a TV or radio station, or Lehman Brothers or Paine Webber, to set the rules? Considering Lehman Brothers' eventual fate—it went belly-up in the financial crisis of 2008—I'm pretty happy with my choice not to let that company set my life's agenda. I set my own rules and am now doing *exactly* what I want! But this freedom came with a price: I was responsible for finding all the opportunities and for bouncing back when there were problems. This took resilience. It took being willing not just to move steadily forward but also to identify and expand the opportunities where I *could* move forward.

The Catch

I've told you what happened to me, but this book is not really about me. It's about: Why not you?

You will have to pose your own version of the question and build a great business around your answer—a business that's just as successful, passionate, and compelling in your world as is the one that I built in my world.

But there's a catch. You have to commit yourself *without reservation* to doing something that you love to do. You can't become truly successful doing something you hate, or by working for someone you don't respect. You have to make a commitment to do what works for you.

The question "Why not me?" is a powerful motivating force in turning commitment into reality. It solidifies your big decision to start a company and encourages you to keep on making the right decisions. Once you make that decision to take control of your own life, once you start to *see* yourself doing something that you actually love to do, you will have more assets on your side than you can possibly imagine.

No More Dreaded Mondays

You know that feeling of dread some people start talking about on Sunday night, when they realize that Monday morning will come in a few hours? If you make the decision I'm talking about, you'll never feel that dread again. I *always* look forward to Monday morning. That's because I'm so grateful and so fortunate to be able to do what I do for a living. Not wanting to show up at work on Monday is an impossibility for me, because of the decision I made about the kind of life I want to lead.

You can make the same kind of decision in your life.

I had the opportunity to take a shot at doing something I love, and I seized that opportunity. Those people I respected told me that if I put my energy behind doing what I loved, the money would follow. And that was absolutely true. When you're doing something you love and are passionate about, the other things fall into place, on your terms.

You really can be in control of your life. Let me be clear, however. This is a big move, the kind most people do *not* make. To make this move you will have to throw out all the excuses, and worries, and "what ifs." You will have to step away from "What will my parents say?" and "What will my friends think?" and "What if I fail?" Instead, your mind-set will be, "Who cares if I 'fail'?" and "I am going to follow my passion, no matter what." Your thinking has to be, *"Now* is the perfect time for me to take my shot."

Isn't it the perfect time? A friend, Tracy Paul, decided right out of college to start a fashion and entertainment PR firm. She didn't even *think* about failing. If she failed, she said, she would try something else—it was no big deal. She didn't get scared at the prospect of failing; instead, she created a successful fashion PR firm (check it out at tracypaul.com) that represents major brands like Coach and Arden B.

> *"*Opportunities multiply as they are seized.*"*
> —Sun Tzu

Why Not Now?

To start this journey, your thinking has to be, "What have I got to lose?" If you're still in your twenties, the answer is almost certainly that you've got nothing to lose and everything to gain!

Take your shot now, while you have the advantage of timing. When I made my big decision at the age of 24 I had limited responsibilities. I was single and living in New York City. All I had to do was put a roof over my head and feed myself. I wasn't worried about 401k's, or retirement strategies, or children. In fact, it amazed me how many of my friends were worried about these things back then, when they were in the same situation I was and settled for jobs. They would change, taking a job that paid a little more or had slightly better benefits, but those changes were just backward career moves. It was as though someone had convinced them they were 45 instead of only 25. Being young and not having too many responsibilities is an exhilarating experience. Take advantage of this time in your life. Being young means having vast reserves of positive energy and enthusiasm that you can devote to your new business. This is a huge benefit, but many young people don't realize how important it is. They focus on what they think they *don't* have rather than what they already *do* have that instantly sets them apart: passionate energy!

Indeed, the very best time to fearlessly harness your energy in support of a new business is when you are between the ages of 18 and 25. That's the time window when entrepreneurs like Microsoft's Bill Gates and Apple Computer's Steve Jobs have started their companies. The energy you have at this time in your life really sets you apart from the older people with whom you will be competing.

Enthusiasm and energy will take you further in business than any other factors. Believe it: Your energy, persistence, and commitment are far more important than your client list (or lack thereof), or whether you've got a huge number of contacts, or how many years you've spent in the industry. These factors are far more important than whether people recognize your name or your company's name at this moment. You don't need twenty years of experience. You can bring your contagious enthusiasm to the table right away and quickly establish yourself as a player.

Do you have a personal computer that runs either Windows or Apple software? The odds are that you do. Now, did those "young upstarts," Mr. Gates and Mr. Jobs, have anything to do with the market achievements that made that technology possible for you? Of course, they did! Do the math: they were both born in 1955. Microsoft was launched in 1975, when Gates was 20; Apple was launched in 1976, when Jobs was 21. They both used their considerable youthful energy to take control of their lives—to overcome fierce competition—and write massive success stories! What would their success pictures have looked like if each had taken five or ten years off to "get some experience" in a corporate job?

Doug Lebda is another great example. He founded the mortgage giant Lendingtree as a young adult, with only his energy to get the project off the ground. After ten years he sold the company to Barry Diller's conglomerate, IAC. Doug has an amazing amount of energy—so much energy and enthusiasm that he runs Ironman triathlons for fun!

Harness the Energy

So, what are you going to do with your energy? Start with a decision! Make that decision now, before you know what your limitations are, and stick to that decision. The "inexperience" you may consider to be your handicap may emerge as a powerful advantage. You don't yet know what can't be done; you may not yet realize its competitive advantage, but remember that it may well be what makes you succeed.

If you're like so many of us, you were constrained by others as you grew up. You were told over and over what you *could not do*. That time is officially over! When most of us hit our late teens or early twenties, we are ready to prove the world wrong. It's time to do just that! And proving the world wrong—or even just trying to—is a lot more fun and definitely more interesting than letting someone else call the shots for you.

Be a Lifter, Not a Leaner

At the turn of the last century, poet Ella Wheeler Wilcox offered her optimist's view of life:

There are two kinds of people alive today,
Just two kinds of people, two only, I say.

Not the good and the bad, for it's well understood
The good are half bad, and the bad are half good.

Not the rich and the poor, for to count a man's wealth,
You must first know the state of his conscience and health. . . .

No, the two kinds of people on earth that I mean
Are the people who LIFT and the people who LEAN!

Wherever you go, you will find the world's masses
Are always divided in just these two classes.

And strangely enough, you will find there are rifts:
There are twenty-plus LEANERS for each one who LIFTS.

In which class are you? Are you easing the load
Of the world-changing LIFTERS who pave their own road?

Or are you a LEANER who lets others bear
Your portion of worry and labor and care?

When you become an entrepreneur, you decide to go down an individual path. You believe, at a deep personal level, in becoming a Lifter, and in not answering to anyone, anymore, ever. You believe in answering to yourself and in building equal alliances with fellow Lifters. And once you enter the Lifters club, no system or person can convince you to join the Leaners.

Leaners take orders. Lifters *place* orders. Which would you rather do?

Maybe you're wondering, "What am I going to need to pull this off?" The answer is simple: a big idea. I'll show you how to recognize that big idea in the next chapter.

"Why join the Navy . . . if you can be a pirate?"

—Steve Jobs

CHAPTER 3

The Big Idea

*"*The entrepreneur in us sees opportunities everywhere we look, but many people see only problems everywhere they look.*"*

—**Michael Gerber, author, trainer, and consultant**

Here's an interesting exercise for anyone considering starting a business: Think for just a moment about the technological advantages an entrepreneur has today over an entrepreneur of, say, fifty years ago. What you quickly realize is that now is an absolutely *awesome* time to start a business. Fifty years ago, if you wanted to find out the most recent discoveries in a field connected to your new company, you had to go to a library or bookstore to find or buy a book or journal on the subject, or maybe track someone down who knew about the subject and convince that person to talk to you. Even so, your acquired information would likely be months or years behind what was actually happening on the cutting edge of the industry. And if you wanted to find out what the competition had done last week, or likely to do next week, you were often limited to blind guesswork. There were no Web sites to visit, no Google searches, no online databases!

If you wanted to identify your best business prospects, or what they were likely doing for a living, or what their favorite entertainments were, or what would inspire them to buy from you, you had to rely on trial and error to figure these things out. You certainly couldn't expect to find your prospects and customers chatting with one another in a virtual discussion group somewhere devoted to a single topic, nor could you expect to join such a group yourself and share thoughts with people who might be reading your words in Boise, or Bangor, or Bangalore.

Now Is Awesome!

Technology has made it possible to learn, create, or do virtually anything we desire, anywhere in the world. We can connect with vast numbers of people, either individually or in groups. The mind-boggling tools at our disposal give us access to a massive array of new and previously unimagined media, to whole new worlds of globally connected prospects and customers. This translates to entire new worlds of achievement, with new doors opening and new maps waiting to be redrawn. There would seem to be no limit to what you could do with a business.

So: Why do some businesses fail? Why don't they all succeed today? After all, these amazing resources are at everyone's disposal. The answer is the absence of *big ideas* in the entrepreneur's world. To get an idea of what I mean by a Big Idea, listen to Kevin Greaney, CEO of Children's Progress, a company that helps teachers and school administrators evaluate how kids are doing in the classroom:

> We were already very interested in student assessment and student achievement. My partner Eugene Galanter had been doing research on these issues since 1984; I had managed several small businesses in the education field. He and I each had some strong opinions about the players who were already out there, these big for-profit publishers who controlled most of the market. They were doing their version of assessment: these big, standardized, bring-a-number-two-pencil, fill-in-the-bubble tests. We knew that those kinds of tests had been developed back in 1906, and they really hadn't changed since then. We felt very strongly that those tests were just boring, that they didn't really tap into the mind of the child being tested, and that they didn't really tell the instructor much. We felt we could build a better tool because we were using principles that weren't, you know, a century old. So we were pretty excited about student achievement, even before we formally started the business.

Kevin Greaney's Big Idea had to do with harnessing technology and research to improve student achievement. He and his partner created a new niche in the field of educational testing. My Big Idea connected the worlds of business and top-tier sports. What is your Big Idea?

The Big Idea

Even if you have access to all of the tools you could possibly need to launch, build, and grow your business, that business will not succeed if you see impossible-to-solve problems everywhere you look. The idea behind your business must inspire you to *notice* opportunities and solutions, and make them big and colorful and interesting.

The Big Idea behind your business must engage you and excite you. It must make it easy for you to reclassify your problems as minor events or bumps in the road—or even as major opportunities. Without a Big Idea to transform challenges into reasons to move forward, your company will perish.

Many young entrepreneurs I talk to are surprised when I mention the importance of identifying a Big Idea that is capable of awakening and inspiring them. They're more used to thinking about ideas that seem certain to connect with customers. A lot of them view their businesses as a trip to the casino: What can they do to place a sure bet? They're likely to talk about how excited the end user is going to be or about the numerical evidence that supports their claim for a certain market.

Numbers are good. Numbers are necessary. And of course the idea behind your business does have to connect with customers. But it's more important to be certain—as Kevin Greaney and his partner Eugene Galanter were—that you're on the right track about something you care passionately about. If it doesn't motivate *you* first, your business is going to be in trouble very quickly.

Is It Really a Big Idea?

Lots of entrepreneurs say, "We're going to take advantage of this amazing market we've found. . . ." Maybe you are—if the idea that you want to connect to the market gets your own juices flowing! If the idea doesn't make you want to get up early and stay up late turning it into a reality, if the idea doesn't make you enjoy doing that, over and over again, it's not really a Big Idea. The Big Idea is what makes you get up and reinitiate the process of building your dream whenever you hit an obstacle. If you don't have that kind of idea, you're not going to get back up when you stumble—and getting back up is what it's all about.

Let me give you an example. The Wild West of Information we now live in can now be accessed without ever leaving the office or home. That's an amazing asset for my business, because we are now selling our services to a worldwide clientele. A decade or so ago, when I started the business, this outreach would have been difficult or impossible. It would have required partnerships and relationships that take years to build, and promotional budgets that we couldn't possibly have put in place. Today we sell sports experiences to people in China, Europe, and Australia. Thanks to the World Wide Web, we are able to target sports enthusiasts everywhere and send people to the World

Cup, big cricket matches, and many other major events that don't immediately spring to mind for the typical American sports fan. We've penetrated markets I wasn't even imagining when I started the business!

But the company couldn't have gotten to this point if I hadn't been a sports fan myself from the get-go. All the information tools in the world wouldn't have helped me if I weren't locked into this business *as a fan*—a fan who understood what motivates other fans.

By the way, the international business started rather slowly, mostly with major golf events such as the British Open. We connected American golf fans who had a strong motivation to see these high-end golf competitions in person, and eventually branched out to other markets, such as the Olympics, for which there was similar interests in American competitors. Interestingly, with global media stirring up more and more interest in sporting events across national borders, we are now sending sports fans from different countries to see events (like rugby and soccer) that they've become passionate about, not from attending events in person but by seeing them on the Internet and cable television. At the end of the day, though, the business is still sports fans setting up trips for other sports fans!

My Big Idea Isn't Your Big Idea!

My company's Big Idea—marketing high-profile sports events packages to corporate customers—was an idea that jazzed me and the people I wanted to work with. There were many things we loved about sports, and it was a cool way to get to spend time with professional athletes. It allowed us to do what we really wanted to do with our lives. And, yes, it was a cool way for us to get to the World Series, the Super Bowl, and the Final Four every year! Sometimes when I think about the business, I ask myself, "Who *wouldn't* find a way to make all that happen?"

That's how I looked at my career (and still look at it) in moments of excitement and passion. Actually, though, I know there are a lot of people who *wouldn't* get up early and stay up late to turn my particular dream into a reality. Yes, there are millions of people who can't understand what all the fuss is about when a big college basketball event like March Madness rolls around every year. That's reality. If you're one of those people—if you simply couldn't care less about sports—my idea for a business would be a lousy idea for you, even if you know there's a market out there.

What Works for You?

You are trying to find a Big Idea that works for you. Don't get distracted by considerations like how big the market is or what the marketing opportunities are going to be, or what features you know for sure that the competition has overlooked. Those considerations are going to be important later on, but right now you want a Big Idea that jazzes *you*, that's capable of making the opportunity look big and bright and colorful for *you*, and that makes the obstacles in your way seem small and insignificant.

Let me boil this principle down even further: if your Big Idea makes it easy for you to see the success ahead and be excited about it before it happens, you've probably got the right Big Idea. If not, you don't have the right Big Idea. Keep looking!

The "Speeding Sports Car" Visualization Test

*"*The entrepreneur is essentially a visualizer and an actualizer. . . .
He can visualize something, and when he visualizes it, he sees exactly
how to make it happen.*"*
—Robert L. Schwartz, author and educator

Let me give you an example that should make it very clear exactly what kind of visualization I am discussing here. It's morning, and you're a good entrepreneur walking to work at your own company. As you walk, you *picture* what you're going to do today. You're excited about what you see in your mind's eye; you are *visualizing* the outcomes you are committed to deliver: the happy teacher and high-achieving student, the trip to the Final Four with a Fortune 100 client, the good things your significant other is going to say about your succeeding—whatever.

As I said, you are a good entrepreneur, so you picture that successful outcome as you walk to work. And, as you walk, you come up with the beginnings of a brand-new idea you could do today that connects to your Big Idea—something that will help you turn that visualization into reality. Well, the prospect of moving forward on your Big Idea has to be so *huge* and deliver such a *vivid and powerful picture* that, as you walk, a sports car could come barreling around the corner, nearly run you over, make you jump ten feet to get out of the way, make you fall to the ground in a heap. And when you pick yourself up and dust yourself off, you are *still* more interested in what you're going to do today than you are angry at the driver.

It takes you only seconds to recover and get back to thinking about your new initiative to support that big idea. Once you know you are safe, you are most concerned about losing your train of thought. Now, for a Big Idea to pass that test, it has to be connected to something you love! Not something you like, not something you're vaguely interested in, not something you're wondering about whether there's a market for. It has to be something you *love doing*—something that cannot be interrupted by a speeding car for more than a few seconds when you are on the cusp of a great idea!

Connect Your Work to What You Love

Look at what the legendary British business magnate Richard Branson had to say on this subject:

> Ideally, since 80 percent of your life is spent working, you should start your business around something that is a passion of yours. If you're into kite-surfing and you want to become an entrepreneur, do it with kite-surfing. Look, if you can indulge in your passion, life will be far more interesting than if you're just working. You'll work harder at it, and you'll know more about it. But first you must go out and educate yourself on whatever it is that you've decided to do—know more about kite-surfing than anyone else. That's where the work comes in. But if you're doing things you're passionate about, that will come naturally.

So, that's critical question number one: What do you love? Now, ask yourself something else: What do you want from that love? For any entrepreneurial effort to work you have to be really clear on what it is you love *and* what you want from that love. Limitless possibilities are no good until you decide which one it is that you love so much, and want so much, that you simply *have* to pursue it.

Unfortunately, most of us can't instantly name a single desire or passion that we know will make us happy. That's one of the reasons people step aside from entrepreneurship: they think they don't *have* such a passion. Yet my experience is that most people who reach this conclusion are only building a self-fulfilling prophecy. They tell themselves that they don't have a passion, and so they never look for or pursue one.

But in fact most people do have a passion of some kind. They have something they love, but they are not willing to figure out what they *want* from that love. For instance, some people are really passionate about sports, yet they choose to see sports as a break from their "real work"—while at the same time using up a lot of energy *wishing* they worked in that world. (Or, even worse, resenting the people who do.) Isn't it better to take that passion and turn it into something you're willing to work *for?*

"I Love This!"

For your Big Idea to work, it needs to be connected to an activity that will let you say "I love this!" and mean it—over and over again. A lot of startup businesses fail—most of them, in my opinion—because the founder or founders picked an idea that wasn't big enough and wasn't personally exciting enough.

Have you ever heard someone say, "I can't believe they pay me to do this?" That's where you're headed now. That's the emotional state that will make your business possible. That's what will inspire you to deal with the logistic, financial, and competitive challenges that will inevitably come your way. That's the way you have to feel; otherwise, *this is not worth doing.* So, if someone else is smiling and saying, "I can't believe they pay me to do this!" why shouldn't that be you, too?

Pat Croce, the owner of the Philadelphia 76ers, was a physical therapist and medical expert for the Philadelphia Flyers early in his career. He loved the work because of his joint interests in medicine and sports. But at the time there were no major business opportunities in a field that was to develop as sports medicine. Soon enough, though, as the extent of medical information regarding sports injuries began to grow and the number of people seeking treatment for such injuries increased, Croce realized an opportunity. He created Sports Physical Therapists, a chain of physical-therapy treatment centers, and he became extremely successful. Croce had turned his interests into a major profit-making operation. Ultimately, he was so successful that he ended up moving from the training room to the boardroom of the Sixers—by following his passion!

Like Pat Croce, you must find a Big Idea that engages you emotionally. This point is so important that I recommend you perform the following activity before continuing to read this book. Set aside a couple of hours with this activity, which will help you develop at least three possible Big Ideas that could launch your business. Then, in the next chapter, I'll tell you what you should do with these Big Ideas!

Identify Your Big Ideas

Consider what activities you could do all day long and hardly realize that any time has passed. What among the things you do puts you "in the flow" or "in the zone"? There's something you know a great deal about already and love learning more about it. Bear in mind that you may not consider this activity or interest to be work as you know it, and that's probably a good thing. What is that activity or interest and what are three possible business ideas that connect to it?

For example, most of us have hobbies, interests, and skills. Look closely at your hobbies and skills, and write down everything you like about them. Then, think of business ideas that connect with these activities. Ask yourself, "How can I turn my love for [for instance, fishing] into a business?" If you think about it, there are tons of ways to turn a love of fishing into a business. Consider the following examples:

- *Love music?* There are great new business ideas that connect to music—all you have to do is find the market! Do a Google search on, say, "classical music." What other businesses already exist to serve classical music lovers? You'll find dozens of them. Which of those businesses do you wish you had started? What industries or associations make you want to be part of them? For example, could you find some way to help great, but not yet famous, classical players take advantage of available technology and the marketing know-how to promote their music online?

- *Love public speaking, and inspiring others with your words?* New business ideas are out there that connect the activities of speaking, teaching, and training to clearly identified audiences. Which of these businesses do you wish you had started? What teaching and training networks do you wish you were part of?

- *Love antique cars?* Antique cars have a huge following, and those people are looking for businesses that cater to their interests. Look for businesses that connect antique cars to collectors. What groups of people obsess about antique cars—and what else are they interested in? Do you wish you were part of this world? Could you sponsor a convention that brought such people together and gave the businesses that marketed to them a chance to sell their wares? Who else is organizing such conventions? What could you learn from how they are operating right now?

Those are just three examples. Don't pick one of these examples, though, unless you're absolutely sure it's right for you. Pick your own passion and start recording your research in a notebook, including up to three possible business ideas.

CHAPTER 4

The First Test . . . and the First Plan

*"*Find a niche market opportunity, exploit it, then reap the benefits while at all times searching for your next niche to enter, move to make, and edge to employ. . . . Find a want, you've found a market. Find a market, then fill the want. Fill the want, you'll fill your wallet.*"*

—Ryan P. Allis, CEO and Co-Founder of iContact

You now have some ideas to test. They may be right for you or they may not—you don't know for sure yet. But you do know that you are generating ideas, and that is the essential first step. What matters next is persistence.

The vast majority of people who start reading books like this one give up after about page five. Since you are still with me, it seems likely that you are along for the long haul—that you are now on your way to becoming one of the people who persistently take action to make things happen in life, and that you are leaving the ranks of those to whom things happen. You should know, then, about the four good things you are about to do.

1. Your business is going to be built on a great idea.

2. That great idea is going to connect you to a market.

3. You will create a plan based on what you learn, on an ongoing basis, about that market.

4. You will adjust that plan over time. (This may be the work of the lifetime.)

That last item is particularly important. Good businesses don't stand still; they don't rely on a single idea. Good businesses adapt to the situations that emerge in the market. Good businesses keep moving forward; they become a *nonstop* source of ideas, not a graveyard for a single idea that once made sense. In 2005, Ryan Allis, whose quotation begins this chapter, was named by *BusinessWeek* magazine as one of the "Top 25 Entrepreneurs Under 25."

Notice his emphasis on initiating change!

REALITY CHECK

Keep an open mind. You must embrace change within your business as it grows, not fight that change. All businesses change as new opportunities emerge—opportunities that you had not envisioned when you started.

The Right Track

Before you can think about change and adaptation, you have to get clear about your own Big Idea. For instance, look at your notebook and consider those three ideas you came up with at the end of the previous chapter. Are you on the right track?

If it's a chore to learn more about the market that connects to your Big Idea, or if you hate making plans about how next to exploit that market, you're on the wrong track. On the other hand, if exploring that market energizes and empowers you—if it feels like something you were born to do, something you wish you could do all the time for entertainment—you are on the right track.

This distinction is incredibly important, worth confirming beyond the shadow of a doubt. I call this part of the entrepreneurial process the "finding out more" stage. It's how you make sure the ideas you are about to base your business on really are the ones right for you. In truth, this is where many entrepreneurs go astray, so look closely at your ideas now, lest you spend months or years with unhappiness.

Many people get sidetracked with technical or market tests at this point in their business development. The following *I Hate Homework Test* is, from a practical point of view, much more important. It separates your best current business idea from every other opportunity on the planet. It allows you to figure out for sure, without a whisper of doubt, whether you've found a Big Idea that resonates for you, an idea you can and should use as the foundation for starting a business.

I Hate Homework Test

Ask yourself this one question, and answer it with absolute honesty: "Does the prospect of finding out more about any of the three business ideas I just came up with in any way feel like homework to me?"

If the answer is yes (or "kind of" or "I don't know yet"), then you have not yet found the right Big Idea for you. You will need to go back to the previous chapter and keep brainstorming. This doesn't mean you've failed; all it means is that you've avoided committing your life to something that will ultimately be unable to make you happy. That's a reason to celebrate. Fortunately, you have figured that out now, and not three or four years down the line, after you have invested huge amounts of money, time, and energy in a business that wasn't right for you. So, keep brainstorming and come up with another three ideas. Repeat the process until one or more of your ideas passes the test.

If, on the other hand, the answer to the *I Hate Homework* Test is, "Never in a million years would I confuse this with homework," or even "I already spent my time finding out more about this, and it didn't feel like homework for a second," then congratulations! You are beginning to get a sense of what your business should be all about. Your business idea has passed the first test.

REALITY CHECK

Never, ever invest time, effort, energy, or money in a business before making certain that the Big Idea passes the *I Hate Homework* Test.

Two Scenarios

Let's suppose that one of your ideas has passed the test. Now, let's move on to the next step—taking that idea further to develop your first plan.

I Love Corvettes

Let's say that one of the three business ideas you came up with connects to your personal passion for Corvettes, the legendary sports car from General Motors that debuted in 1953 as the first all-American production performance vehicle. As it happens, you've got a Corvette; it was a gift from your rich uncle Cory for your twenty-first birthday. You're a huge fan of the car, and you have studied its history closely. You have a strong sense that somewhere, somehow, your interest in Corvettes could translate into a really great idea for a business.

Indeed, you've made a pilgrimage to the National Corvette Museum in Bowling Green, Kentucky. Also, one of your goals has been to own a fleet of Corvettes, one from each decade of the vehicle's production. You set that goal for yourself about five years ago. Your Uncle Cory has a vintage 1965 Corvette, and one of your most treasured memories was the time he let you drive it.

That's the situation. Now, suppose I were serving as the coach who would help you launch your business. Suppose I were to ask you, as your coach, to take an hour to find out more about Corvettes and the hundreds of thousands of people who love them. Suppose I were to ask you to use that hour to learn as much as you possibly could about the car's extraordinary base of devoted fans. Suppose I told you that this hour would be an important part of what comes next in your life and that it would help you find your niche and build the plan for your business.

Would your reaction be, "Do I *have to?*"

No! If you were someone who was already intensely passionate about Corvettes, you'd jump at the chance to learn some more about how this car has attracted its huge fan base. You'd probably say, "An hour? Is that all? Why don't I take all weekend? That way I could really get some insights into this community of people called 'Corvette fans' and why they're so connected to this car. Give me two days—I'll let you know what I figure out on Monday morning."

That's what it was like for me when I started to find out more about the world of professional sports. If someone had told me to research the sports-event industry for an hour and then stop, I would have begged for more time! I loved—and still love—all the action that accompanies a sporting contest. The more I experienced in that environment, the more I read about it, the more I wanted to learn. When I went to a football game, I wasn't just a participant; I was studying. I saw how the pre-game tailgate parties worked, who was organizing them, and how they drew people. It fascinated me; I learned how the hospitality opportunities were set up, and I figured out who was paying for what to make them happen. I asked a lot of questions of the people working the venues (or, for that matter, on site attending these functions), and each answer led me to a new question. I loved finding out about this stuff!

I Guess I'll Have to Research Corvettes

Now let's look at a very different situation. This time, you don't have a personal passion for Corvettes. You never *have* had a passion for Corvettes, or for any car, for that matter. You have never ridden in a Corvette. In fact, as a direct result of your rich uncle Cory's obsession with Corvettes, and his annoying habit of talking about the cars endlessly during family get-togethers, you really don't much care for Corvettes.

The truth is, the whole sports-car thing leaves you cold. Sports cars strike you as gaudy, inefficient, expensive, and, perhaps worst of all, environmentally irresponsible. You're quite concerned about climate change, and the idea of someone driving around in a forty-year-old vehicle that gets about nine miles to a gallon of gasoline, and being proud of that, makes you feel just a little bit disgusted. What would happen to the planet if *everyone* suddenly decided that it was cool to drive around in a Corvette? You don't even want to think about it.

But, wait. You mentioned to your rich uncle Cory that you were reading this book and that you were enjoying coming up with ideas for new businesses. You also mentioned that you were hoping he could help critique your business plan. When you said that, Cory got all worked up. He grew enthusiastic about the possibility of helping you start your new company. In fact, Cory told you he would invest $100,000 in your business—*if* you started a business that was devoted to detailing and repairing vintage Corvettes. He's absolutely certain there's a huge market for this service.

Cory announced that he was now your business coach. He told you to invest one hour of your time in finding out what turns otherwise normal people into Corvette fans, and he asked you to report back to him on Monday morning so the two of you could discuss what the business launch might look like.

Now what is your reaction? In this scenario, how likely are you to put off everything else on your schedule so you can figure out exactly what goes on in the mind of a Corvette owner? Let's be honest. If there weren't $100,000 to consider, you're not likely to put this learning at the top of your list. Even *with* $100,000 to consider, it feels like a bit of a stretch to you. You are much more likely to say to yourself, "Okay—I promised Uncle Cory I would put in an hour and let him know what I figured out about Corvette owners. It would be great to have $100,000 to start the business. I guess I should put in the hour. I guess I have to research Corvettes."

STOP! Uncle Cory may have $100,000 to give you, and he may be absolutely right about the market for Corvette detailers, but *this is not your business*, and it is, therefore, not your best choice. There are lots of people who make poor career and business choices based on input (or pressure) from relatives or peers. Don't live someone else's dream! If your best friend thinks you should be a doctor, and talks to you endlessly about what a great doctor you'd be, you may start think-ing he must be right. You may start thinking about how much money doctors can make. You may start thinking about how important doc-tors are to society. You may start thinking about anything and every-thing *except* whether you would actually enjoy being a doctor! Instead, take the *I Hate Homework* Test. If you always feel like you're doing homework when you're finding out what it takes to be a doctor, guess what: you shouldn't be a doctor! (Or, at least, I don't think you should be *my* doctor!)

Once you have passed the *I Hate Homework* Test—once you are eager to learn more about the Big Idea for your business because it matters to you personally, and doesn't feel like an assignment you have been given by someone else—you are ready to start looking around, doing research, and building your plan.

Who Are You Helping?

The chance to help a specific group of people should be one of the major characteristics of your business idea. I mentioned Kevin Greaney, of the firm Children's Progress, in the previous chapter. Here's what he had to say about developing his company's mission:

> We felt strongly, based on our own experience in the field, that there was a whole market niche in the world of educational assess-ment that no one was looking at, which was teachers who taught pre-kindergarten through second or third grade. Everyone in the industry was looking at the grades above that. We knew we could develop a better, more interesting, more helpful assessment system

for schools to use with younger kids, and we also knew we could give teachers more information about what kids knew, what they don't know, and *why* they don't know it, if they didn't know something. We knew we could give teachers in that underserved group some insights about what they should do about that situation, when a child doesn't know something. That was our niche.

Greaney connected his dream of helping teachers achieve better results with the students with his idea for better assessment tools. So as you access your business ideas, be sure to pinpoint your interests. Then, for each idea, figure out the specific group of people you would be helping. Once you have a strong sense of who those people are, your "job"—actually your privilege—will be to spend time to find out as much as you can about those people, their world, and how your big idea connects them to you. Find out all you can! Connect with everyone you can!

Luckily for you, you can learn a tremendous amount about your industry almost immediately and without leaving home by means of the World Wide Web. You'll quickly glimpse what is happening in it today, and this learning will energize you and excite you about the prospect of following through to the next link, the next article, the next business that seems connected to yours.

So much good information is out there, on the Web and elsewhere. You can read industry trade journals, attend trade shows, and call people in your chosen field. When you invest the time to find out more by making direct connections with others in the field, you will quickly discover that people like to talk about themselves and to share their insights and opinions about the industry. It makes them feel important. So call them up, explain that you're trying to learn more, and listen. Most people will feel honored that you care about their opinions.

You should also try to find mentors, or people who have experience in your area. Speaking with someone with field experience can help you choose the best path. Search out family, friends of family, and anyone you have come across who seems to have business knowledge. But make sure that the field you're asking about is *your* passion, not just theirs!

Vince Gibson was one of the first people to sell sports travel packages to the corporate crowd. A former head football coach at Louisville and Tulane, Vince realized that there was always a demand to go see his teams play on the road. In fact, he started this business when I was still in grade school. To say he had more experience with and knowledge of the business than I did when I started would be a serious understatement.

Vince was not your typical business competitor. He was always willing to answer my questions honestly and openly, and he offered advice to a young man starting out in a business that was directly in competition with his. He became one of my mentors; I would call him up and ask him questions about the business and where the opportunities were to be found. I always make an effort to be open and honest, and helpful to others who are starting out in the same industry, because of the great way Vince treated me when I was coming up.

As you talk to people in the field, try to get a clearer picture in your own mind about your particular niche or potential product angle. You should be coming back, again and again, to the all-important question: Who would I be helping with this business? In fact, it is essential to have a specific focus when you are starting a business.

You'll eventually find that focus, and once you do, you will make the commitment to become the very best player in your chosen niche.

The professional poker player Phil Gordon offers a great example of how to build a top-tier business in a niche market. Phil is a remarkable guy; he's one of only five people in the world to both come in first in a World Poker Tour event and also finish at the World Series of Poker's final table. But Phil found his niche in teaching people about poker rather than playing it. Notice the transition: He identified a group of people who could use the information he had acquired about his passion. He then built his empire based on writing books, creating DVDs, and starting a production company that teaches people about poker. Phil was able to target a particular segment of the market and capitalize on it. Check out Phil's world at www.philnoli mits.com.

Start the Plan, Whether You're Ready or Not

With your target audience in mind and your niche clear, you next develop a game plan for your business. Trust me, this plan doesn't have to be an elaborate business-school project (although those certainly have their place; even though I didn't go to business school, I know a lot of great business leaders who did). Just outline what you want your company to do and how you want it to look. Jot down your best ideas on a single sheet of paper.

I drew up my first business plan out on a single sheet of paper. Many successful businesses have been created on the backs of envelopes or on paper napkins. The main point is that they all had a specific focus. Your simple game plan will be revised and updated many, many times, but you should start it *now*.

A simple game plan should include:

- Your best idea so far for a name for your business.

- Your best description of the group of people your business will be helping. For example, these might be corporate leaders who are eager to solidify relationships with key customers and employees by taking them to the Super Bowl. Or superintendents of school systems who have to make sure students are ready to perform at an outstanding level by the time they take standardized tests in the fifth grade. Or people who want to play poker the way it's played by the best players in the world.

- Your vision of what the company will look like five years from now. For instance, how many employees it will have, how much money it will be pulling in, what your personal salary will be.

- Your main goal to accomplish in the first year of your business. This goal should be specific, measurable, attainable but a stretch, realistic, and tied to a specific date.

- The three most important immediate goals you see for your business to achieve in the next thirty, sixty, and ninety days that will support the big goal you just identified.

That's the starting point—that single sheet of paper. You will, of course, move on to list step-by-step goals that support your major goal.

You must be able to visualize your company growing in the way that your one-page game plan suggests. Think positive! Use the one-page plan to see clearly how many employees you will have in five years, how big your personal bank account will be once you have implemented this plan, and so forth.

Of course, you'll want to follow your own instincts in drawing up the game plan, but I've included here (on page 47) what my initial one-page sheet looked like, back when I was launching my business. Customize this one-page plan as you see fit.

Revising and updating your game plan will become the work of a lifetime, but again and again you will come back to your basic vision of your business. The main point here is that you start the plan by putting it down on paper; that way you will have no doubts about the direction your business will take. You may draw up your vision for the business on a paper napkin, but you will need a more detailed set of plans to turn that vision into a reality.

Don't try to create all the elements of that detailed plan right now, but be ready to budget time at least once a month to measure how close you are to meeting your big goals. I recommend reviewing your step-by-step goals at least once a month, though you may want to do it as often as once a week. Whatever schedule you choose, be sure you have plenty of "reality checks" that help you confirm you are moving closer, not further away from, your basic goals as stated in this game plan. . .

Remember, too, to be ready to adjust your plans. Building a business is like running a marathon, and a marathon is run one step at a time. The course may change over the months and years, but you need always to concentrate on the short-term goals along the way to the

① get (lawyer / accountant).
② read books on own company / industry
③ computer training.
④ get adweek backs / sports backs for ideas —
⑤ call Brett G.

I ① Selling Sponsorships for pre established events
A. ex. US Open →
Greater Hartford Open →

① work with event people + with companies

B. create niche ideas for sponsors
ex. Nestle ~~Candy Shop~~ Dunk
Pepsi "Big Slam" contest
① Talk to Pam's contact about consulting
② meet w/ company + present many diff events to them (Binder of sponsorships)
consult with them for best
4 events to Sponsor/ sponsorship.

II. ① Selling Spons Packages Through other companies

A. Nestle NBA → let O Putney's group handle it.
B. N.Y. Knicks packages
C. NY Rangers packages
D. call teams + leagues (Season packages) from NFL/NBA
E. Umpires club / NFL / NHL /
company based all over won't availability to all teams not
one package deal. Different teams through NBA.
ex. Timberwolves, Bulls / Phoenix — companies strong cities get
tickets only for those arenas.
*call wolves person — Dana

III. ④ Player appearences — call nicely friend — local front end product
endorsements
② corporate parties   call him ask about
③ Motivational speakers → Mike Singletary (ex) setting up any
(Team NFL motivations)
④ NBA Retired players
① appearence companies +
② league   *   video instruction
③ merchandise (shirts with legends pictures) +(sell retail)
players on front - lifetime stats on back of shirt
⑤ Player product endorsements →
⑥ ~~...~~

finish line. Having long-term goals is important, but you will need to create, critique, and revise short-term goals consistently in order to reach those long-term goals. In the end, short-term goals are what will lead you to achieve the long-term prize. And both the short- and long-term goals should support your Big Idea.

"There will come a time when big opportunities will be presented to you, and you've got to be in a position to take advantage of them."

—Sam Walton, Founder, Wal-Mart, Inc.

CHAPTER 5

The Partner Principle

*"*A healthy business partnership is comparable to a marriage, built on a solid foundation of trust, respect, and understanding.*"*

—**Stephanie Ciccarelli, entrepreneur; co-founder of Interactive Voices, Inc.,**

and nominated for Canada's Young Entrepreneur Award in 2006

You put yourself at a huge disadvantage when you assume that you can start a business on your own, without the advantage of a business partner who is your peer, rather than your employee. It's an equally huge disadvantage to make a snap decision when it comes to choosing that business partner. In fact, the selection of your business partner is one of the most important decisions you will make in your entire life—not just in your business life but in your whole life, period. As Stephanie Ciccarelli suggests, "When two complementary business people come together to form a company, guided by the same vision and values, they are at the very heart of their corporate family, and nurture the business as parents would their children."

REALITY CHECK

Startups that feature two people who come together regularly to make important decisions have a significant competitive advantage over businesses in which all the major decisions are made by one person, who never consults a partner.

Businesses that are partnerships have owners who see more possibilities, avoid more problems, and respond more effectively to crises. I call this inescapable business reality The Partner Principle. Why put yourself through the stress and insanity of going it alone? Think of it this way. You will spend most of your life at work. If you are starting a business, your life can be consistently great if you choose the right partner, or it can be consistently awful if you choose the wrong partner—or no partner at all.

So, wouldn't you want that advantage, too? But just how do you go about finding a partner?

The Perfect Pair-Up

You might assume that picking a business partner is similar to making an important hiring decision. Actually, it's dozens or even hundreds of times more critical than that. If you make a bad hire, you can let the person go. It may not be a lot of fun, and there may be roadblocks to terminating that person, but you can do it and the next day you can move on. On the other hand, if you build the business around the wrong person, your business, your reputation, your vision for your future life, and even your physical and mental health, could suffer in ways that may be hard for you to imagine at the time you're starting the business.

At the same time, some people use prior bad experiences with a partner in a business that failed as reason to avoid finding any business partner for a new enterprise. But the real lesson to learn from a business that failed is *not* that a partner is always too risky, but that the partner you chose was the wrong partner. Choosing the wrong partner will doom your enterprise.

The closest analogy to picking the right business partner is not the act of hiring the right employee, but the act of picking the right spouse. I hope, for your sake, that you wouldn't get married after having just a couple of good conversations with someone. Similarly, I hope you won't pick a business partner based on a few superficial exchanges or a couple of promises or flashy compliments.

This really is one of the most important decisions you will ever make. Don't skip it, and don't make it lightly. According to Ciccarelli, "A co-founder needs to be a good communicator, a person with whom you have synergy, and a friend." My advice: *Find someone who compensates for your weaknesses.*

I know a lot of people who decided, in their twenties, to put off having kids in order to start a business. These people tend to think in "parental" terms about their companies, even saying things like "It's my baby," or "It's like I'm getting this kid ready to go off to college." They're not talking about a future child they plan to have; they're talking about the companies they've built from scratch and are now moving to the next level.

The parenthood/marriage metaphor is worth remembering over time. The idea of parenthood helps you focus on the *relationship*—the partner you need to have in order to do your job as well as it can possibly be done. Assume that a child is about to enter your life. Which would you rather be: a single parent or a parent involved in a committed partnership with someone you trust and respect?

I'm not saying that it's technically impossible to launch a success-ful business on your own, but finding someone who brings to the table strengths that you don't have will greatly increase your chances of staying sane, balanced, and intent on your journey.

What to Look for in a Partner

You should look for someone with whom you have good chemistry—someone who fills in your blind spots, does well doing what you don't do well, and who always tells you the truth. Typically, a good partner makes a shared commitment to the business, envisions shared rewards that are clearly defined, and offers sharply differing perspectives and skill sets. You should look for a partner who offers all of that.

By the way, *all* successful business partnerships are based on this idea of taking different perspectives in a discussion and having differ-ent talents. If you are tempted to pick someone who has similar or identical skill sets to the ones you bring to the business, someone who never or hardly ever challenges you, step back and take a break. You are on the wrong track. You need someone whose main purpose is to *complement* you, as in "to complete the picture, add the missing pieces to the puzzle." You want a good relationship, of course, but not someone whose main purpose is to *compliment* you, as in "to flatter you, tell you you're wonderful, and repeat all the things that you want to hear." That latter kind of partner will kill your business.

Two Heads Really Are Better Than One

I always wanted to have a business partner because I knew that two heads really are better than one. I knew that I didn't possess certain traits and that I would need to look for those traits in a partner if I wanted to create a successful business. I talked to a number of people before finding my long-time business partner. I'm sure some of the people I "auditioned" are now shaking their heads, since we recently sold our business to a private equity firm. In the end, I was lucky enough to find a partner who was the perfect counterbalance to me— someone whom I had known for a long time and had a good personal relationship with already.

I have been fortunate to work with an extraordinarily honest, hard-working, and committed partner. Without my partner Brett Sklar, I certainly would not have written this book. He has been with me every step of the way and has put as much into our business as I have. We have been through all the wars together, all the good times, and all the not-so-good times.

Brett was the ideal partner for me because his skill set complemented mine. I tend to be the optimistic, wide-eyed idea person and

Brett is able to conceptualize things and offer a game plan that can get us to where we need to go. He is a tireless worker, a dedicated and moral businessman, a generous boss, and one of the smartest people I have ever known. He is honest—an extremely important quality in a business partner—and modest to a fault. I am blessed to have worked with him over the past decade.

I remember meeting Brett the first time while he was at the University of Arizona and Michael Kahan, a friend I grew up with, was his roommate. We played a game of basketball and really hit it off. Mike had class, so I was alone with Brett that first day. I could tell right off the bat that he was a good person. Little did I know that several years later we would go into business together and form a lasting friendship.

Brett, who'd grown up in L.A., decided to move east after college and was looking to go into his own business. It just so happened that Mike once again hooked us up. Brett understood my vision, shared my passion, and signed on. He saw the opportunity and took it when nobody else would—at a paltry $600 a month! Mike donated his old computer so we could start the business. (He got a nice thank-you check years later, when Brett and I sold the business.)

You deserve a partner as great as mine. Don't you?

Other entrepreneurs have great business partners with whom they share—and create—terrific, energizing dreams about starting from scratch and building something magnificent. Other entrepreneurs have partners who respect them, push them, and challenge them to achieve the highest possible level. I certainly have that kind of partner. Why not you?

The Classic Partner Profile

Business partners can operate in many different ways and still achieve success together. A lot of "classic" partnerships have one person who is a visionary and can see where the company needs to go and the other who is the nuts-and-bolts person with a practical road map to get there. These two personalities sometimes translate into an outside sales–type personality and an internal operations–type personality.

For instance, it's likely—not mandatory, but likely—that as your relationship with your business partner gets started, one of you will have the vision for where the business should be one, two, and five years down the line while the other will develop the details of the plan that will turn the vision into reality. One partner will be an extrovert who loves connecting with people and talking with them about the business while the other partner will be introverted and prefer avoiding sales and networking responsibilities.

Likewise, one partner will be good at creating and pitching "big ideas" while the other partner will have the skills that support internal logistical goals. One partner will tend to be more optimistic and "possibility-focused" while the other partner will think more conservatively and throw a spotlight on the potential downside of a given course of action.

One partner will have strong creative-thinking skills while the other partner will have strong analytical or problem-solving skills. One partner will focus on what's taking place outside of the organization, interacting with prospects, clients, and/or vendors, while the other partner will maintain an internal focus that supports what's happening inside the company.

For example, my father had a successful trimming business with his brother for over forty years in the garment district of New York City. My father was the classic outgoing salesman who would bring in the business; his brother was the office manager who would run the operations. Without my father there would have been no customers, but without an internal person like his brother, they could never have successfully managed all the business that came in. The two halves operated successfully as a whole. My father was smart enough to realize he needed help in certain areas after he started the business and therefore offered my uncle a very good opportunity.

Partners Give You a Second Opinion

Having someone to bounce ideas off of and give you a second opinion can help you keep your sanity. In starting a business, you'll face some extremely tough days, and being able to share them with someone and talk through situations are essential.

REALITY CHECK

Looking for a second opinion from someone you trust is not a sign of weakness, but rather a sign of strength. Every entrepreneur I interviewed for this book had someone with whom to discuss difficult situations before coming to a decision. You should, too.

At one point in the development of our business, I was convinced that we should pursue three or four extremely exciting new strategic opportunities—simultaneously. One of them was an initiative to take the business online. This opportunity came about in the late 1990s, before the dot.com bubble had burst. Basically, I was the voice of *Go for it!* That's the kind of person I am. I want to do a lot of different things. I felt that it was time to redefine our business and reorganize it into a bunch of different types of businesses, and I wanted to do that all at the same time. I wanted it all, and I wanted it now!

My partner Brett, though, was there to offer a second opinion. He's always been good at helping us to keep our focus and stay closely connected to the methods that have helped us establish our market niche. He saw the potential value of the big initiatives I was pushing, but he also saw the value of keeping us grounded and focused. His opinion was not that we should discard all my great ideas—in fact, he saw a lot of potential in them. What he recommended, though, was that we slow down and take things one at a time. He gave me a dose of reality by saying, "Look, Rob—why don't we pick one of these things?" He made sure we did something well with one idea before we jumped ahead with other ideas. The bottom line was that, at this time, it wasn't the right time for us to take our whole business online. And, believe me, I'm very glad today that he had that alternative perspective and was willing to share it with me frankly.

Things wouldn't have happened that way if I hadn't chosen my partner with great care years earlier. So, too, you should take care in choosing a partner. The specific things I was looking for, and found, in my partner were:

- Fine character and high moral values

- High energy level and the ability to work long hours

- A degree of passion for and commitment to our business that matched my own

- A skill set that complemented mine

- The ability to tell me things I didn't want to hear

- The personality to maintain a good relationship with me

Picking the Wrong Partner Costs Too Much

There's a TV game show during which people are hooked up to a lie detector and told to answer embarrassing questions truthfully—with the reward for truthfulness a huge cash prize. You've probably seen it. On one show, the host asked a contestant, "If you knew with absolute certainty that no one could ever possibly find out what you had done, would you rob a bank to solve your family's financial problems?"

The contestant answered yes and won $10,000. The audience cheered.

I don't know about you, but I wouldn't want to do business with someone who has that kind of value system, and I certainly wouldn't pick that person to be a business partner. As a budding entrepreneur, your job as you consider potential partners is to find out who would answer affirmatively to a question like that—without actually submitting the person to a lie-detector test. After all, a lie-detector test isn't really a great rapport-building option when it comes to interviewing prospective partners!

A friend of mine started what became one of the most successful restaurants in San Diego. At first, though, the business was struggling. Every night the place was packed, but my friend was mystified. He didn't understand why, at the end of the month, he was always losing money. He soon realized that one of his business partners was skimming cash from the till. I don't know how much his choice of a dishonest partner ended up costing him, but whatever the number was, it was too much.

REALITY CHECK

You must have a clear sense of what your partner's morals will and won't permit. You can't *think* you know what your partner's values are. You must *know for sure* what those values are.

There are ways you can identify, and rule out, people whose personal ethics are going to be bad for your business. For example, take your prospective partner golfing or out to a restaurant. See how that person interacts with others; watch how well he or she treats service people. Ask your prospective partner about his or her friends, family, and major life experiences. You can learn a lot about people by listening closely to how they describe relationships and events.

Your partner should *not* be:

- Someone you would not unhesitatingly trust with the life of your closest blood relative

- Someone who is "just like you"

- Your spouse or significant other (there is too much risk that one or the other relationship will suffer)

- Someone who has never told you an uncomfortable truth or is uncomfortable doing so

- Someone whose resume is great, but who doesn't have the ability to build rapport with you or others

- Somone your instincts tell you is not the right person

Indeed, *don't ignore your instincts!* As Kevin Greaney, CEO, explains,

> You can have a degree from Harvard Business School, get the best books in the world, and you've still got to make the decision based on your gut when it comes to picking your business partner. . . . At the end of the day, you've got to ask yourself, "Can I do business with this guy? Do I trust this guy?" It's a matter of having a gut feeling. I think picking a business partner is really more of an ethical and moral decision than a business decision. Somebody might have all the academic credentials in the world, or all the seemingly relevant business experience in the world, and things still might not work out. You have to have an internal sense of whether it is right for you to pick this person.

How does this person treat others? That's an important question. You need to know if this is really the guy you want down the hall from you as you launch your business. You can have the best finance guy in the world, he can run numbers all day long, but if he consistently mistreats people, then you have to ask where else that problem is going to show up.

Like any relationship, a partnership requires work. Taking on a business partner is a big decision and, as I've emphasized in this chapter, it's one that should be given a great deal of thought, time, and energy. If you invest that thought, time, and energy, and follow your own best instincts, you will find the right partner.

Even when you pick the right partner, there will be occasional disagreements and arguments. Some days you will wish your partner would just go away and leave you alone. If you have done the right work upfront, though, those days will be few and far between. Again, this relationship is a lot like a marriage. If you respect the other person, tell the truth, and make it clear that you are willing to listen, you will both end up being glad that you entered the partnership.

And here's a final word of advice. Don't ever leave the office for the day upset about something that has to do with your partner. Talk things over. Always let your partner know where you stand on a business issue and make sure you understand your partner's position. Once you know where each other stands and why, and can respect those positions, you can go home for the night!

CHAPTER 6

Gut Check: Getting Started

"Never, never, in nothing great or small, large or petty, never give in except to convictions of honor and good sense. Never yield to force; never yield to the apparently overwhelming might of the enemy."

—Winston Churchill

At some point, the rubber hits the road. And that point is likely to be during the first year of your new business.

There are a lot of books out there offering "expert advice" on starting a business. They come to this point in the discussion and go into great detail about the "how" of getting your business off the ground: the logistics, the funding issues, the research, the supplier relationships, the structure, the attorneys and accountants, the software, and so on. Usually, these "experts" are indeed experts about the *externally observable processes* that apply to your business. Those factors are important, of course, and I don't want to pretend that expertise on these subjects is not going to matter. However, those processes are only part of the equation—and not the most important part.

Ben Sturner, founder and CEO of The Leverage Agency, a major sports sponsorship and branded entertainment company, recalls the time he met that critical moment in the life of his new business:

> I was working out of my house and making phone calls, and I remember the biggest concern was having my first employees, and making sure we made payroll every time. I was doing this all on my own without any outside funding whatsoever, and there were plenty of deals that I made at what I would have to call the twenty-third hour. My philosophy is that, if you keep pushing and keep believing in yourself, it will all work out.
>
> I remember there was a time, and it goes back to the very beginning of my business, when I barely had enough money to travel to go on a trip that I absolutely had to go to in order to meet some sponsors. That was a big decision. The conference was sixteen hundred dollars, and I had two thousand dollars in my bank account. I decided to go to Chicago and do the conference. As a result of that

decision, I got a big deal with Reebok for a five-year, multi-million dollar deal that really launched the company.

I met them at this conference, and I know, absolutely know for sure, that I wouldn't have met them if I hadn't had the guts to go to Chicago without any money. I did it because I was hungry. When you're working for yourself—owning your own company—is when you really get hungry.

Ben's story is about the time the "rubber hit the road"—for him. What would have happened if he hadn't put almost every cent he had behind that trip to Chicago? Who knows? The point is that he got on the plane. And you will have to, also, at some point early in the game.

How vs. Why

Decisions about externally observable processes, such as what accounting software you choose during your first month in business, are part of the *how* of doing business. As important as they are, they will probably not make or break your company during its critical first year. As someone who has been through that first year, I can tell you there's a much more important issue: the *why* of starting your business.

You can learn about the *how* of business and, if you choose, delegate that task to someone else. But the *why* of business is for you and your partner to figure out. And it's going to be personal for each of you. That *why* is a reflection of the internal journey that every successful entrepreneur will navigate. The *why* answer leads you safely past what I call the "gut-check moment." And that moment is inevitable.

Ben Sturner's story captures the moment perfectly. He had to decide to commit funds he did not have—he had to take a risk. It's a test of your gut feelings that you simply cannot avoid. So don't even try to avoid it; instead, figure out the *why*.

What's for Sure

I don't know anything about you. I don't know anything about your business idea. And I don't know anything about the customers you are trying to reach. But I definitely know this: There will be a "gut-check moment" early on in the life of your business, and if you don't know *why* you are doing what you are doing, you will make the wrong move and your business will miss out on an opportunity.

The real point at which you start your company doesn't happen when you give it a name or sign some legal papers. The real moment comes when you know why your business is worth taking a "punch to the gut" for—and you act on that knowledge. If, like Ben, you are empowered by thinking that it's finally your show, that it's all up to you, that you're hungry enough to do what is necessary to succeed, then you do what Ben did and use your *why*! If your *why* helps you pass the "gut-check moment," then you know you've got the right *why* for your efforts!

Remember, this is the part of launching a business that most books and programs don't explain—or even mention. Every successful entrepreneur has had an early moment when the decision had to be made whether or not to go to Chicago. That moment is not likely to be something out of the ordinary; but it does happen to all young entrepreneurs. And it is going to happen to you.

The "gut-check moment" is not a decision you can avoid with careful thought or postpone, or talk your way out of. It's an important, inescapable part of launching your business. Yes, there will come a point when you have to make a decision that proves to everyone (including yourself) that you believe completely in what you are doing and that you are willing to expose yourself to short-term risk and pain in order to secure a long-term benefit that you truly believe you deserve. Before that happens, you haven't really started your journey—or your company.

Fear and the Entrepreneur

These "gut-check moments" are scary, yet a lot of the books on entrepreneurship and the training programs describe them in vague terms, minimize them, or skip them entirely. Why would the authors of these business books do that? Usually it's not because they're irresponsible or uninformed; it's because they have a professional obligation to teach their readers, and they have read or heard that fear impedes the learning process. The "experts" don't want to scare the reader. They want to support the learning process, and that means finding ways to make the process of starting a business approachable and doable. That's fine. It *should* feel approachable and doable. But the truth of the matter is that starting a business is also going to feel scary sometimes, and you need to know that upfront and be ready for it.

For people who are truly committed to becoming entrepreneurs, encountering a little fear upfront is probably a good thing because overcoming fear is a big part of what they're going to be doing. That's why I've given this subject a whole chapter in this book. So let's take a closer look at fear itself.

Were You Scared?

How did you feel when you read about Ben's "gut-check moment"? Did your stomach clench up a little bit when Ben mentioned how much money he had left in his bank account? That was just what that feels like.

Did you find yourself hoping that you would never find yourself in a situation like that, or vowing that you would do anything necessary to avoid having to make a choice like the one Ben had to make? Those wishes and desires are normal. They are nothing more or less than part of starting your own business.

Believe me, the sooner you pass the "gut-check moment," the better off you will be.

What Options Are There for Facing Down Your Fear?

Think about it for a moment: What choice do you have? If you don't make that critical decision when the situation arises, which will almost certainly occur during the first twelve months of your business, you'll just be putting the "gut-check moment" off until the next time it comes along. And, more important, you'll delay the point at which you can actually learn to deal with such moments!

That's what happens to the vast majority of (would-be) entrepreneurs, by the way. They focus on planning the *how* of the first twelve months—often in an attempt to make absolutely sure that nothing like what happened to Ben could ever happen to them! Not only is this a waste of time, since what happened to Ben is going to happen to any young business, no matter how carefully planned, but it gives an unrealistic expectation of what running a business is all about. It makes young entrepreneurs think they can remove fear from the equation.

There is no removing fear from the equation. You can only learn how to *respond* to fear. You will never learn what it takes to face down the future scary situations that your business will present until you learn the *why* that allows you to handle that first scary situation. You will recognize that facing down and overcoming scary situations is a big part of what you will be doing for a living. In exchange, you are building a future so big, so much fun, so tightly connected to who you are and what you are becoming that it helps you overcome those fears time after time.

Some people think of entrepreneurs as fearless, but starting a business is *not* a matter of never feeling scared. Most entrepreneurs know this, and some will even say it out loud. True entrepreneurship means knowing what to do, and why, when you *do* feel scared. That's a skill you are going to master in the months and years to come. Indeed, you *must* master it. You can't be an entrepreneur otherwise.

Let me tell you about one of my "gut-check moments." Very early on in our business, we had sold a client packages to the Major League Baseball All-Star game in Colorado. I still remember that the cost for us was $25,000. A few weeks before the game, my supplier called me to tell me that he was going bankrupt and could not deliver the tickets. This was a smack in the gut if there ever was one.

At this stage of our business, $25,000 meant the whole year's likely profit. I knew that I couldn't go to my client or my reputation would be ruined. Luckily, we were able to piece together other hotel inventory and other ticket inventory and make the program work after many, many days of panic, fear, and stress. We lost money on the deal, but we had a happy client who never knew what we went through. I learned a lot about myself from that experience. For example, I learned that when it comes right down to it, I am going to do the right thing—and do right by my clients—regardless of the profit or loss on an individual deal.

Why This Is Important

I focus so much on the *why* here because there will come times when you will ask yourself, "Is this worth it? Why is this happening to me? Why am I doing this?" You must have an answer for these questions!

Indeed, there will be tough days ahead when you think to yourself, "Gee, it would be so much easier if I got a regular job and didn't have to hassle with this whole start-up business idea. I've only got two thousand bucks in my bank account! How can I possibly go to Chicago?" These doubts usually come during a tough day when problems seem larger than they are and you've talked yourself into believing that everything is going wrong. It's okay; every entrepreneur has moments like that. If things never got tough, we would live in a world of extremely successful individuals who had never put the work in to achieve at the highest levels.

So, what does the *whole* picture look like? At these moments you have to step back to get some perspective and look at *all* the opportunities and *all* the resources. You have to refocus on your own best answer to the *why* question. If it helps, you can do what I do: rephrase a question. Instead of "Why is this happening to me?" ask yourself the more empowering question, "Why not me?" The answer to this second question gives you the *why*: Because I deserve this and I love the field! If the answer you give yourself resonates for you, you can work through the problem. This, too, will pass.

A wise person once offered this advice: Assume the feeling of the wish fulfilled. That is, when times get tough, disengage for a moment and feel how it is to be successful with your business. Tell yourself you are going to be successful, no matter what is happening at the moment. *Feel* what it feels like to be successful once this storm has passed. Act as if you already are successful. This "acting as if" feeling makes it easier to overcome obstacles and achieve success.

Don't Replace Fear with Fear

Some people try to replace one fear (say, the fear of losing money) with another fear (the fear of failure). They think things like, "If I don't go to Chicago, I won't be able to prove to my dad that I'm really a success after all." The fear of failure can motivate you in the short term, and may actually keep you going during some tough times, but it has limits as a long-term motivating force. Something tells me that Ben Sturner didn't bet sixteen hundred bucks on his business because he was afraid that he was going to fail. He was betting *on* something, not *against* something. You should, too.

Fear of failure cannot be the *why* you rely on when you encounter your "gut-check moment." This kind of fear freezes people in their tracks and holds them back from ever taking any risks. You cannot be afraid to fail and also be successful in business—it's that simple. Business is all about overcoming failures and obstacles to create character and success. Every successful businessperson has "failed" at something in the past, and that failure turned out to be precisely what made them better at what they do now.

Yes, the people who are able to pick themselves up off the mat are the ones who ultimately succeed. Everyone gets thrown down. But the people who win are the select few who know how to get back up. So, accept that failure is okay, and ask yourself, "What's the big deal?"

Here's another "gut-check" story. Jennifer Walzer started Backup My Info, a technology-storage company. Initially, Jennifer encountered some very tough obstacles with her business. For example, once she lost her biggest client owing to the client's merger with another company; that meant Jennifer faced the prospect of a huge revenue loss for the year. The new company that acquired her client let her know that they already had a data-storage company they were quite happy with. "Gut-check moment!"

Jennifer insisted on meeting with the client, just to finalize the separation. She called them once a week for three months, and she finally ended up securing what was supposed to be an exit meeting. But notice what she was doing as she made those calls: demonstrating her obsessive commitment to taking care of her clients! When Jennifer did meet with the client, she didn't disappoint. She was able to make the decision makers at the new company realize that her service was in fact better, more helpful, and more cost-effective then their current one. She rescued the account!

It's no wonder Jennifer's company is a big player in the data-storage industry today. After all—the whole company is based on her own answer to the all-important question: Why am I doing this? Here's Jennifer's take on that critical question, and notice how she frames that issue for herself and others:

> We provide small and mid-sized businesses with a completely auto-mated data backup service. That's what we do. But the reality is, *why* we do what we do is more important than *what* we do. We have a passion for taking care of people. There are a lot of data-backup companies out there, but what makes us different is that we built our company around this belief that we want to take incredibly good care of you. So we're more of a boutique backup service, where we hand-hold you every day, making sure that your backups run smoothly. If we see any problems, we call you. That's the whole obsessive nature that we have, to make sure that you're protected.

That's *why* Jennifer bounces back. That's *why* she's in business. She's got a passion for taking care of people.

That's Jennifer. Why are *you* going to bounce back? Why are *you* in business? What are *you* going to fall back on when you have your first "gut-check moment"? If you don't know, you must find out!

Your *Why* Blocks out the Negative!

The *why* you are doing your business must get you past the inevitable "gut-check moment," and it must also block the naysayers you will encounter as well as all of their negative energy. In fact, dealing with naysayers is a good way to *practice* dealing with your first "gut-check moment" before it arrives. That means naysayers are really a blessing in disguise!

Negative people can only tell you what you *can't* do. These people are living in fear, so stay away from them! Detach from these people because they will only project their own fears onto you. Talk to any entrepreneur with a successful business; you won't hear fear in that person's voice.

Of course, detaching from negative people is easier said than done. You may be related to a naysayer or trapped in a meeting with one for an hour. If you ever find yourself thinking as these people think, it is your personal responsibility to refocus on *why* you are growing your business. If you can't do that, you will not be able to get your business off the ground. Period.

I could have filled this book with stories of people who were heavily invested in convincing me that I was crazy for leaving Lehman Brothers to pursue my passion. Now I have to ask: Which would have been crazier, and riskier? Doing what I was born to do? Or sticking around at Lehman Brothers—which is now out of business—out of sheer force of habit?

Do not listen to anyone who is similarly invested in convincing you that you are crazy or that you are making a mistake. Believe in yourself. Replay repeatedly your *why* for starting the business, and get ready for your "gut-check moment." It is, without doubt, on its way to test you. Now, at least, you will recognize it for what it is!

CHAPTER 7

Priorities for That First All-Consuming Year

*"*They say there are three types of people: some make things happen, some watch things happen, and others wonder what happened.*"*

—**Walt Frazier**

To become the kind of person who makes great things happen by launching a company, you must make a big personal investment. I'm not talking about money (yet). I'm talking about time. I'm talking about three years of your life—with the tone for those three years set by the things you focus on ten to sixteen hours a day, six or so days a week, during your first year in business. During that first year, you are going to be doing a whole lot of breathing, eating, and dreaming your company. There is no way around it.

Setting the priorities for those first twelve all-consuming months is what this chapter is all about. You need to understand, however, that even if you do make that critical first year work for you, you are really going to be devoting three or more years of your life to your business idea. You are probably in your twenties or thirties now, and you will be making a conscious choice to devote these precious years to your cause, your mission.

To be perfectly frank, this commitment will be easier to pull off if you don't yet have major family or relationship commitments. It's certainly not impossible to accomplish this with a spouse and family also looking for your attention, but for most people, the demands are too conflicting. It's much easier to launch the rocket that is your new company when you can devote most, if not all, of your time and attention to the effort. Regardless it can always be done if you commit yourself to the cause.

It takes a massive effort and a great amount of energy upfront to get a rocket off the ground. That first burst of rocket power that gets the ship off the launching pad is like the first year of a new business. The point when the ship leaves the earth's atmosphere and enters zero gravity is like the two years that follow that first year of a business.

It's a demanding ride, and it will take you a while to reach the point where you have the systems and procedures that begin to make it feel like the business is in orbit.

If all of this seems a little intimidating, that's probably good. You should realize the demands upfront. You may be better off finding something else to do. But if you honestly want to know whether you have it in you to launch a successful company, if you are certain you've found the big idea around which to build your life and company—and you don't want to go through life regretting that you didn't give it a shot—then get ready. We're talking about three years of work requiring what most people would regard as prohibitively long hours and excessively high energy levels. Only you can say whether the effort is worth it.

REALITY CHECK

This is your shot. This is the time when you find out if you've got something worthwhile. Make this commitment to yourself before you make a major life commitment to someone else.

As I mentioned in Chapter 2, I had a limited number of responsibilities at the age of 24. By deciding to go for it, to take a chance on life, I assured myself that I would never look back in twenty years and say, "What if?" For me personally, that would have been the real failure. So, if you're still with me, congratulations. You know you've got the right idea, or at least the right kind of idea. You are ready to set priorities for your first year. And you are ready to give it everything you've got for at least the next three years. Then, if necessary, you can reassess. But during those first three years, you need to commit fully!

Your priorities, your commitment to the business, during the first year will affect everything else that happens during the life of your business. This is why I focus so closely on first-year priorities. If you can keep your eyes on the prize during this first year, you'll be more likely to make the following three years work. Just as your personality shapes the business, your commitment to the priorities you have set in the first year shapes the commitments others will make to your company. A halfway commitment during the first year will be reflected in the culture of your business. You'll have a halfway business.

Let's look at an example. When Kathy Sharpe was starting a technology design shop called Sharpe Partners, I tried to persuade her to join my company and start a tech design division for us. She had been working for a big player in the industry at the time, and I knew she'd be a valuable addition to my team. But Kathy said to me, "You know, I want to see how things go on my own first before joining a company again." I admired her attitude. She was giving it a shot—devoting part of her life to the fulfillment of her personal dream. She set benchmarks for herself; if she reached a certain point and concluded that what she had wanted to do hadn't worked out, she could easily get a job, maybe even with my company. But she had a dream, and she wanted to see what would happen with it. I respected that.

Seven Priorities for a Successful First Year

As it turns out, Kathy built her one-person company into a powerhouse of the tech design world. Today she employees a multitude of people and works with major Fortune 500 brands on their technology branding. But Kathy set priorities and then *went for it* during her first years. You can, too.

Here are the seven priorities you will want to set for yourself during the first year.

1. Build a Culture of Action and Enthusiasm

You want to build a company that rewards taking action, a company that is perceived as being youthful, vigorous, forward-thinking, and results-oriented. In the very early days, you will face a lot of competitive hurdles, a lot of questions about your experience, and a lot of questions about your client list (or lack thereof). The best—and probably only—way to overcome these obstacles is to make up for your lack of a track record with vigor and energy.

People expect action and energy from the young, and they are likely to search out young and hungry companies. You will find that clients are willing to pay for your energy and dynamism, and they will even take a bit of a risk in order to get young, energetic minds on their side. They will give you a shot when they see that this is what is driving you.

I'm sure there are successful companies that have been started by young entrepreneurs who took the opposite course—companies that were built on values of maturity, deliberation, caution, and in-depth, multi-level analysis before anyone in the organization did anything of consequence. The problem is, I can't think of any of those companies, and I doubt you can, either. People don't go to young, new companies to get delaying tactics and sober, cautious advice. They go to old companies for that kind of help.

So, how do you show youth and energy? During your first year, find reasons to take action. This is your primary competitive advantage. If you start looking around for reasons *not* to take action, you'll be in trouble. Be proactive, not reactive. Take the initiative!

Likewise, find reasons to reward your people for taking action. Find ways to reward their energy and enthusiasm. In particular, this is a huge competitive advantage that many young entrepreneurs don't realize will set them apart from the older organizations they are competing against.

Enthusiasm and energy will take your business further than any other factor. You don't need twenty years of experience to have contagious enthusiasm; you can put enthusiasm to work for you at almost anytime, and in virtually any setting. One of my favorite examples of this is an Indian entrepreneur named Suhas Gapinath. At the age of 14, he was at the gates of the Indian Institute of Science in Bangalore; he wanted to attend a seminar for CEOs on the educational system in India; a security guard stopped him and told him he couldn't get in without proper ID. Suhas said, "I don't have my ID card, but here are the business cards of the people I know." The security guard made a few calls, and Suhas made his way into—and eventually addressed— the conference! Today, in his early twenties, he is the president and CEO of Globals Inc., an IT company.

2. Take Daily Action on Your Business Plan

What separates successful entrepreneurs from floundering entrepreneurs? Daily commitment to fulfilling the benchmarks you have set for yourself and your company in both your short- and long-term business plans. In short, you have to identify the things you're doing that are moving your business forward, today, in a measurable way.

Even with modern technology, things don't happen overnight. Businesses usually take years to form, but those years are the result of a disciplined system or process that someone is putting into practice each day. Every day you have to be willing to put your time in and do what you know needs to be done. For some people, this daily commitment means picking up the phone and making ten sales calls a day, no matter what. For others, it means creating ideas for new products, new systems, or new marketing initiatives, and then carefully testing the results. For yet others, it means conducting daily status meetings with the team and troubleshooting what's happened since yesterday and what hasn't.

There is some daily routine that is right for you—a routine that matches the benchmarks of your business plan. Your job is to find that routine and hardwire it into your world. Ronn Torrosian, the owner of 5W PR, is a good example of this principle. Thanks to Ronn's tireless daily work ethic, 5W is ranked by several major trade publications as one of the fastest-growing PR agencies in the business. Ronn is a tireless worker, and with sheer dedication and work ethic he has built up 5W in a relatively short period of time. His sweat equity is, I think, the primary engine of his company's growth.

As for my daily routine, I make sure to get some intense physical workout just about every working day. That daily exercise habit might take the form of a tennis match or a basketball game, but whatever, it's essential to my outlook and my success. I find I am more productive on the job when I feel physically fit. What's more, I am more optimistic about work (and life) when I've worked out recently, and that optimism makes a huge difference when it comes to generating business opportunities. *How I feel, and what I'm expecting, definitely affects the conversations I have with stakeholders and prospective stakeholders!* There is no denying that this habitual focus on demanding the most from myself, day after day, is a big part of what has made me successful in business.

During your first year in operation, you're going to figure out what has to happen each day to make sure you're taking care of your baby properly. And just like a parent, you'll eventually conclude that taking care of yourself is an important part of taking care of your baby.

3. Get Your Web Site Up and Running

Your Web site has to say "This is who we are" to the outside world, and it has to be compelling. You can get great results without spending a lot of money for Web design just by looking for a young and hungry Web designer who's looking for a shot, as you are. If you don't have the HTML or design skills in-house, don't attempt this job on your own. But do have a clear sense of the image and feel you want your site to convey.

Expect to update your Web site regularly and to improve it constantly over time. At the time we launched our company's Web sites, these sites were only just becoming a promotional must for companies. I knew that I wanted a site that was user friendly, one that people would want to spend time visiting and come back to. With a top-of-the-line site, I could make my company look and feel like a billion-dollar company. I knew I could offer better services than some of my competitors, who were extremely large companies at the time. But I had to get the client to put my company on the same level as those competitors, and to conclude that we were the right choice, capable of handling a big project.

A Web site that is outdated, with irrelevant or months-old information, is a real deal-killer. It makes your company look stagnant and gets people thinking that you aren't on top of things. If they see graphics that are out of date, how do you think they are going to view your ability to stay on top of their account? It is imperative to keep an up-to-date image.

However, while getting your Web site up and running is a major priority for your first year of operation—you certainly won't be taken seriously without it—don't imagine that getting the Web site right will answer all your marketing challenges. Nor should you allow building or critiquing the Web site to suck up all the energy and resources you have. During your first year in business, do the very best you can for your Web site with as much as you have now—and be ready to update and improve on a regular basis.

The Resources section at the back of this book lists some ideas for launching a great Web site.

4. Talk to Absolutely Everyone About What You Do

Who says opportunity stops at five o'clock? You need to always be talking about your business, as well as thinking about it constantly. Remember, you are building a brand for your company. In the beginning, you will likely be the only mouthpiece, and if you are not successful getting people interested in what you are doing, no one else will be getting people interested, either.

It should become second nature for you to talk to people about your business at parties, at family gatherings, and at outings like sporting events. Consider every person a sales opportunity, even if he or she might not ever be the end customer. You never know who the people you meet might know or might be speaking to next. You want people to be ready to mention the great conversation they just had with you.

Think of this as doing publicity, or PR, on a small scale. Why wouldn't you use your personal network to get the good word out about your business? Word of mouth can be a big positive; one-on-one connections lead to greater visibility for your business, which leads to customers.

So, during the first year, you must be perpetually marketing your company, yourself, and your products or services. So much of what people buy is based on perception. It is your job to make people perceive that your product or service is the best fit for them. Seize every opportunity; look for every new avenue to grow your business and start connecting. You may sound like a broken record, but trust me, soon enough it will pay off.

Marketing yourself at this stage, when you might not be able to afford a PR firm, means picking up the phone and calling reporters to let them know what you are doing. Reporters are always looking for content, as they constantly need to have stories to write about. This is a great way to get your name out there and develop some credibility early on. If you can get your message into the media, you will have a great advantage over competitors.

Use that youthful reservoir of energy you have to talk endlessly about what you love most about your business. After all, you are venturing out after something you are passionate about, something that will drive you. We all have this energy when we are young and starting out. Do not hold back or bottle this up. Share the feeling with the world. Let everyone feel your passion. Don't be scared to make it known how excited you are or how much energy you have for doing what you are trying to do. After all, if you are not passionate about what you are doing, then you cannot expect anyone else to be, either. Make it known to the world how you are here to change it.

5. Try to Fund It Yourself, or Mostly Yourself

Lots of entrepreneurs ask me, "What type of funding will I need to get my business off the ground?" I always advise would-be business owners to go after the least amount of funding that is necessary. Sure, it feels good to say that some venture-capital firm invested millions of dollars in your idea, but a few years down the road, when you are doing well, it will not feel so great to know that you own only 25 percent of your company.

The best sources of initial funding are probably (1) your own savings, and (2) family and friends. You have to be comfortable going to certain family and friends who you know are in a position to help you. Friendship and family are more important than business, so tread lightly; you do not want to put yourself in a position that might ruin a good relationship. Especially, I would go this route only if you know the investment will not severely impact the lender. Credit card accounts and banks can also be good sources of money when starting a business, but you should talk to your financial adviser. You need to look for the cheapest options and find ways that will not burden you with unnecessary debt.

As for our business, we financed ourselves as we went along, starting with less than $10,000, and plowed revenue from sales back into the business! At first, no banks wanted to lend us money. We ended up deciding that we didn't need the funding because we were fortunate enough to have good accounts receivable, thanks to our in-house financial person, Andy Robb. (You'll learn more about Andy in Chapter 15.) When we were doing well, all the banks came knocking on our door, eager to find ways to lend us money. That's a common story for a lot of companies that decide to self-finance.

The reason I recommend self-financing for people who are just starting out is that fixating on some outside source of capital is a great way to make launching the business someone else's responsibility. You don't want to do that. If you spend the entire first year talking about presentations so that someone else can take action or make decisions, your mind-set is wrong.

Never forget: When you start your company or venture, *you are the business*. That means you are in charge. When I started my company, I was using my own money, which wasn't much. I did not have a computer, but I did make sure I had my own letterhead. I worked out of my apartment, which of course became "Suite 1905" instead of Apartment 1905. I had a separate phone line installed. I printed my own business cards. And no matter how amateurish the documents may have looked, I knew I was in business with my own money. I felt—and still feel—immense pride in everything that came as a result of that very humble start.

You may reach a point, after the first year, where you decide that, for strategic reasons, it makes sense to bring in some outside funding. But that's a later stage. Don't spend your first year looking for funding instead of finding customers and delivering great results. During that first year, *be* the business. Do everything you can to fund it yourself and use the inevitable cash-flow pressures as motivation to track down customers.

6. Get Connected, No Matter What

During your first year of operation, it's extremely important to develop new relationships and meet people in your industry. I was fortunate enough early on to meet Alex English, the former Denver Nuggets Hall of Famer. Alex gave me a shot at having my first office when he asked me if I wanted to share an office with him near Madison Square Garden in New York City. Alex had a player-representation company with Tonja Ward and Tammy Houston. He made me feel like a winner right away, and he respected what I was trying to build.

You can't just wait for those connections to happen. You need to spread the word and get out there, one way or another. When I was starting, I would sit in my office and make over 100 cold calls a day to potential clients. I had the same pitch that I would say over and over. Soon enough Alex and Tonja would jokingly recite the pitch to me, verbatim. Getting connected was all about living and breathing the business. Those cold calls produced a seedbed of clients, and from that seedbed my company grew.

7. Stay Balanced

During the first year, and all years thereafter, you will have to find a way to achieve balance. Basically, this means avoiding the temptation to work seven days a week, eighteen hours a day, without a break. Indeed, you *have* to give yourself a break, even though Priorities 1 through 6 are daunting.

You need an outlet of some kind—a hobby or exercise activity that helps you stay sane. Many nights I left my office at 10 P.M. and went to the gym to hit the heavy bag until I had alleviated all my stress. If you are working hard and putting all your energy into your work, you are going to need a release. I found exercise to be the perfect remedy for the stresses of a long work day, but something else make work for you. Everyone needs some time off to maintain balance and perspective. You are no exception.

So, anything that can get your mind off the work for a set time will help. A major talent agent to well-known actors and actresses plays basketball five times a week; his work is so intense that he looks at these times on the court as meditation. In my case, I joined a group called Trilife, founded by two friends of mine, Ross Galitsky and Scott Willet. Their big idea was to start a company that would train people for Ironman triathlons. I relieved my stress with hours of biking, running, and swimming. It was the perfect relief and for two years I got myself into pretty good shape—and even completed two Ironmans, as well as a ton of great road races. I also made life-long friends.

Ross and Scott are the perfect example of two friends who started a business doing something they love. Their energy and love for triathlons made Trilife such a huge success. After only a few years in business, their jerseys and jackets seem to be everywhere in New York City. Their business is thriving—thanks to their desire and their passion!

Expressing passion for what you do as an entrepreneur is not just your right—it's what you do for a living! In fact, there will be times when you have a special responsibility, in your capacity as owner and founder of the business, to express that passion by taking a special kind of leading role in the promotion and marketing of your business. We'll look at that issue in depth in the next chapter.

CHAPTER 8

You Are the Company

"I don't like asking for money. However, when you are truly passionate about something and have a lot of faith that you will succeed, it's worth it.**"**

—**Razor Suleman, CEO, I Love Rewards**

As I mentioned in Chapter 5, there are some great business partnerships that allow one person to take a more active role in the sales and marketing arena for a brand-new business and another person to assume a more passive role, perhaps focusing on internal concerns like product development or administration. This two-person division of labor is a good model to consider when you launch your company.

If you are the "outside" partner, this chapter is of particular relevance to you.

The Heart and Soul of Your Business

In every book about launching a business there's usually a chapter or two that discuss the "how to" of marketing; that is, how to position your business in the minds of prospective customers. There's also a chapter on the "how to" of one-on-one sales; that is, how to start conversations with prospective customers and how to close the deal. Some books combine the two activities into one discussion, but they always seem to focus on the "how to." They give you a lot of steps to follow and pass along a lot of checklist-type advice from experts. For a long time, I wondered what it was about these chapters that kept me from believing them. I think I've figured out what it is.

Those chapters in other books about launching a business almost always talk about the *how* of marketing and selling, whereas my brand of entrepreneurship is, as you've probably figured out, always focused on the *why* that drives these activities. I am all about focusing on the goal—and on the *reason* for moving forward toward that goal.

It's not that the *how* isn't important. It *is* important, once it works for you. But the best entrepreneurs are routinely focused on the goal, the *why*, that drives them to connect with customers that they sometimes have a hard time telling you when they have stopped selling. *Everything* they do connects to selling.

You could even argue that this is an essential part of the development of any business: the entrepreneur's ability to *internalize* sales and marketing functions, and to start performing them (or delegating them to others) more or less automatically as opportunities arise. This may happen in a dozen different ways within the span of a single hour in an entrepreneur's day. So, it's a mistake to think of selling your business as a job that starts at point A and stops at point B. No, it's something that drives you all day long.

Sales That Grow Your Company

For entrepreneurs, there is no right or wrong way to sell. If you have the passion and the enthusiasm for your product, and if you find ways to connect with people, your energy is going to come across. Sure, you will have to "ask for the business" and learn to say things like "Where do we go from here?" and "What happens next?" and "This really makes a lot of sense to me—what's your take on it?" Ultimately, though, it's a mistake to adopt someone else's selling system. It's better to just reach out to as many people in as many different ways as you can, and discover what feels most comfortable for you.

People who tell entrepreneurs about how to sell and market are likely to produce one of two reactions. The first, "I wouldn't sell or market like that," is a totally valid reaction because entrepreneurs do tend to sell with a very different style from most other people. The second, "I'm already doing that, or some variation on that," is usually on the mark, too. The point is that *any* attempt to impose an external system on yourself is probably a mistake. What you do to sell and promote your business has to be a reflection of what you are already willing to stay up late for and get up early for. It has to connect to your *why* and be part of your own experience.

If you are tempted at this point to ask yourself, "When can I stop selling?" ask yourself a different question! It is a mistake to think of sales or marketing as subjects that start at a certain point and end somewhere else. A bigger and better question to consider is: "What would broaden and improve on what I'm doing right now, and would allow me to reach even more people?"

Start with Your Own Personality

Entrepreneurs *are* their companies, which means they are different from everyone else in their organizations who sell and market. For the entrepreneur—for people like you and me—selling and marketing the company is personality driven and really personal. Who else in the organization can say that?

Your personality, by definition, is going to send some powerful messages to everyone you talk to about your business. How could it be otherwise? So that's where you should start. Embrace and accept your own personality, and avoid the trap of trying to sound or think like someone else.

> ## REALITY CHECK
>
> When it comes to personally marketing your business, the first commandment is to Be Yourself. Do not try to be anyone else; do not try to alter basic parts of your own personality in order to "sell it."

Your personality is going to determine any process or checklist that may emerge as your company's distinctive way of marketing or selling. And since your personality is omnipresent, you should accept that, in a very real sense, you will never stop marketing or selling. If you pause to think about it, you will realize that you have been selling all along; now you are directing your no doubt biased, emotional, and personally skewed version of what works into new and bigger channels.

Look at the question again: "What would broaden and improve on what I'm doing right now, and allow me to reach even more people?" This question will link up with the *why* that is already driving you. So forget about any *how*. Look for ways to broaden and improve what you're doing now.

Entrepreneurs *must* approach sales and marketing in a way that takes full advantage of the force of their personalities, which is, in most cases, also the personalities of their companies. In the early phases, that's going to take the form of a *personal guarantee* from you to the prospect.

My Story

In one of my very first face-to-face meetings with a potential client, I shook hands with Art Niosi, who worked in sales and marketing for

Ocean Spray, the juice company. I could tell Art was concerned about my ability to perform after seeing how young I was. I had spent weeks building up a great rapport with him over the phone, trying to sell him on using my company to run a complicated promotion around the NCAA Final Four, for which Ocean Spray was a sponsor at the time. I was excited that he took the meeting with me, but also disheartened to learn within five minutes of arriving that he was also meeting with another company on the same promotion.

I knew it was going to be a tough sell. I couldn't sell my company's past performance because I had absolutely no prior track record in the business. I could only sell myself and my word. And so I gave Art my word that, if he worked with me, I would run through walls for him to make his promotion a success. Art was tough; he grilled me on every detail of the promotion and on my ability to deliver certain components. I was careful never to promise anything that I couldn't deliver, but I got as energetic and intense as I possibly could about what I knew *for sure* that I could deliver.

When it was all over, I wasn't at all sure that what I had done had been enough, but I knew I had told the truth. I walked out of that meeting disappointed, thinking I was never going to get a chance to prove my worth. You can imagine how surprised I was when Art called me that afternoon to tell me he had decided to split the contract and give both companies a piece of the work. He said he had admired my perseverance and trusted what I had told him. He respected me when I gave him my word, and he had been impressed by my honest answers about what I could and couldn't deliver for him.

While we didn't get all of the business, it felt good to know that someone had put his faith in me regardless of some initial concerns about age and lack of past performance. Art became a long-term client over the years, and we developed an extremely trusting relationship. In short, I got the business from Ocean Spray because I was willing to put myself on the line—and back up what I'd promised.

Razor's Story

Here's another great story of someone who did the same thing. Razor Suleman launched a business that eventually became Razor's Edge, and, thereafter, I Love Rewards, a company that *Maclean's* magazine recently named one of Canada's Top 100 Employers, and that *Profit* magazine cited as Canada's 12th Fastest Growing Company.

If you're starting a business, it helps if you love what you do. Back when I was fifteen, I loved sports cards. My love of sports cards is what taught me my first lesson on raising financing. I started collecting sports cards as a hobby when I was 12. Nothing was more exciting to me than collecting and trading sports cards. When I learned that I could actually earn money doing what I loved, I made the move from being a collector to a dealer very quickly. But *how* I made that transition is worth looking at. It was a formative experience for me.

At the time, Upper Deck Hockey (UDH) Cards were about to be released, and I knew it was going to be hot. If I could just get a couple of cases wholesale when they first came out, I could sell them for a quick profit. I soon learned that getting my hands on UDH was not going to be easy. Once I looked into it a little further, I discovered that the application process for becoming an authorized dealer was extensive and that I had to be a legitimate business in order to get approved.

I was not going to let a little thing like an application process get in the way of my passion. I "positioned" myself—creatively, some might say—in such a way that I more or less brought my business into existence on the spot. Much to my surprise, a few weeks later, I got an official letter from Upper Deck congratulating me on my approval as a dealer. Even more surprising was that I had been allotted 20 cases of UDH cards.

My journey was only half over. The second roadblock I ran into was that I needed $18,000 in capital upfront. I had a little money saved from delivering newspapers but that was only about $3,000. I went to the person I was closest to, the person who has always believed in me, my mom. I told her how great this opportunity was and how I would have all 20 cases sold even before they arrived. As always, my mom was very encouraging and supportive—but she didn't have the money.

You see, I grew up in a very traditional household and my dad controlled our limited funds. Growing up, I learned that there were three things my dad was not generous with: affection, recognition, and money. Today, as the head of a major business in a competitive industry, I've secured a million-dollar line from a very conservative bank and received a multimillion-dollar term sheet from a tier one venture capitalist. But I have to admit that asking my dad to borrow $15,000 was probably the most difficult meeting I have ever had.

I told him everything I had told my mom. I told him all about my plan to buy $18,000 worth of sports cards. I told him why I was so certain that the cards would be sold to buyers before they arrived. I included my one-page business plan (it was more of the cocktail-napkin variety). And I told him when I would pay him back. I was surprised when my dad agreed to finance my venture.

With my certified check in hand, I couriered my order to Upper

Deck. Less than a month later, I got 20 cases of UDH cards. As per my plan, I flipped them to my network of retail sports card dealers for a tidy profit, and repaid my father. I was left with a nice little pool of capital with which to continue financing my future ventures. The experience taught me a lot about the importance of bootstrapping. I reinvested the capital from my first endeavor to finance my next. I've used this strategy throughout my entrepreneurial career and it has allowed me to take my $3,000 in seed capital and build it into a company that is now valued at approximately $10 million.

There are a number of things I want you to notice from Razor's amazing story. First and foremost, notice that the *why* was always what drove his process. He loved the idea of getting paid to work in the industry he loved. As a result of that *why*, which was his unique motivator, he kept trying, kept looking for new ways to move forward, kept improvising. When his mom couldn't say yes, he didn't appeal to a book or an outside expert for advice; he called his own next play at the line of scrimmage, which was to move on to his dad, even though he could have found plenty of reasons *not* to do that if he'd wanted to look for those reasons. If that meeting with his dad hadn't worked out well, Razor would no doubt have called another play and tried something else, until he'd tracked down that $15,000 in working capital.

Second, I want you to notice how selling was a constant in Razor's story, even though that selling connected to other issues. He had to sell his mom and dad on the idea, and of course that dovetailed with some family issues. He had to close the deal for an additional $15,000 in capital, which certainly qualifies as selling, but securing seed money also has to do with things like finance and accounting and operations. He had dealers to begin relationships with and keep happy; that connects to both sales and customer service. Razor's job *started* when he secured the money he wanted—it didn't end. Once you *are* the business, you lose the right to bail after the sale. Everything connects, and you are connected to everything.

Third, notice that Razor moved quickly from someone who liked his idea but couldn't make a decision—his mom—and made a direct appeal to someone who *could* make a decision—his dad. He didn't ask his mom to make the presentation for him; he decided to get "face time" with the person who could give him a yes or a no, quickly. This is a classic trait of entrepreneurs who sell. They don't keep calling people who don't actually move them forward; they don't stay bottled up in one place for long. They find a way to keep moving forward!

*"*High achievers spot rich opportunities swiftly, make big decisions quickly, and move into action immediately.*"*

—Robert H. Schuller, pastor, and author of *Move Ahead with Possibility Thinking,* among many other bestsellers

What Else Works?

There is a simple, very powerful, and very flexible sales tool that you can easily adapt to your personality and your *why* for starting your business. In fact, you can use it right now. If you employ it effectively, it will deliver great results in virtually any industry. It's called picking up the phone and calling people.

I mention this tool because it's been my experience that people who aren't *willing* to pick up the phone and call people to talk about doing business also don't make good selling partners. If you are having a problem doing this yourself, you may want to reconsider your role. I've seen businesses disintegrate because nobody wanted to be the person responsible for generating business.

Marketing your own firm by phone is among the simplest, most cost-effective, and measurable strategies available to you. There may be some startups that wouldn't benefit from this sales tactic, but there can't be many. Other marketing tools can complement this one, but none can replace it. So, *pick up the phone!*

Calling Techniques

You have to make your calls from a position of absolute certainty. *Why* are you calling? Not too terribly long ago I was making phone calls to top company executives to introduce my business to them. You can call these conversations "cold calls" if you want; I looked at them as ways to create relationships with people who could benefit from the experiences we could deliver—people who could help me create a great business in the industry I had chosen for myself. They were only cold calls if I failed to build any connection or rapport with the person, and that didn't happen very often.

My cold calls really didn't sound like cold calls. They were more like calls from one sports fan to another. If I was calling New York, I dug around a little bit after introducing myself, so as to figure out whether the person I was talking to might possibly be a Yankees fan or a Mets fan or a Celtics fan. Establishing that "safe" moment— when the person realizes he can talk to me about sports—was pretty much my goal for the first call. If I got the call to that point, and could get the person to take my call next time, I was happy.

Once I had built up a little rapport, a bit of commonality, I could find out something about the person's business and *briefly* start to share stories about clients with similar interests whom we had helped to build events. Making a good emotional connection with someone on the first call was fairly easy for me because—let's face it—*I was the business*. If I couldn't have a good phone conversation with someone based on how the Yankees, Mets, or Celtics were doing, who could?

Of course, most calls don't turn into a business deal within a few minutes. You try to build a network of contacts, not wave a magic wand over someone to turn the person into a customer. *There is no such magic wand.* You tell a short success story that genuinely excites you, find out if there's a possible match, and figure out what, if anything, the prospect thinks should happen next.

I read once that it takes something like ten to twelve phone calls and/or meetings to move a buyer from "Who is this?" to "You've got a deal." Who knows if that's accurate? What I do know is that, if you sound scared or like you're trying to follow somebody's process, you will never get past "Who is this?"

In summary, the idea of reaching out to people and talking to them about what you do *must* energize and excite you. The idea of getting bad calls out of the way so you can make the next good call had better not frighten or intimidate you. If one person had an argument with her spouse last night, and then gives you a hard time over the phone, don't put yourself on trial. Move on. The next good call is waiting for you. Likewise, set a goal for the number of good calls you want to make each day. Track those calls for six to eight weeks, at least, and measure how many of them turn into business opportunities or referrals for you.

What Else Works?

There's a tiny guitar shop on 48th Street in New York City called Rudy's Music Stop. It is legendary for finding, building, selling, and servicing electric guitars of the highest imaginable quality. The proprietor and resident guitar freak is Rudy Pensa. Today, Rudy's customers include John Mayer, Green Day, Velvet Revolver, and U2, among many other top-tier musicians. Now that's good word-of-mouth!

Here's Rudy's advice on personal marketing: "If other people already provide the service for the business you're going into, be sure you set yourself apart." And that's pretty much the story of Rudy's career. As an ambitious, high-energy twenty-something, Rudy set himself apart from the "big guys" in New York's highly competitive, geographically centralized "guitar Mecca." He did this in three ways: stocking (and, eventually, creating) higher-quality guitars; providing deeply personalized, one-on-one service; and offering a family-style atmosphere that the stuffier, more traditional guitar outlets would never have dreamed of allowing. When aspiring (or current) guitar heroes walk into Rudy's shop, they're encouraged to sit down, have a cup of coffee, relax, and strum the merchandise before they make a purchase. They're also encouraged to talk guitars with the master. He pretty much *lives* to talk guitars. That may not be the personality of the person who's in charge of one of the competing stores in the neighborhood, but it definitely is Rudy's personality. Rudy's personality—and his enduring love affair with guitars—is what drives the operation and what has allowed him to build up a series of relationships with some of the most prominent names in the world of music. Rudy's final piece of advice on the matter: "Reputation is more important than money."

Exactly the same concern drives Pam Paspa, proprietor of a very different business: Paspa Physical Therapy. The company's marketing philosophy rests on essentially the same principle, however: get it right, face to face, and generate good word of mouth. Pam started her physical therapy business as a one-woman operation, and built it up on the strength of her own—and, eventually, her employees'—superb person-to-person relationships with patients.

> In our business, it's the patient who does the marketing for you. You have to make absolutely sure the patient is satisfied. It only takes one patient who complains to a doctor to destroy a major source of future referrals for us. So we do a lot of listening. I would tell entrepreneurs who are just starting out not to get distracted by the word "marketing." In the end, it's really relationship management. That's what builds your reputation.

An online testimonial about Paspa shows the power of word of mouth: "I've gone to Paspa for three different periods over three years. The staff is almost uniformly warm and friendly, the equipment is up to date, the physical therapists span the range of styles from cautious to aggressive, allowing the patient to work with someone who fits their speed and style, and the one-on-one care is great. I went to other places near where I live and they were so poor by comparison that I am back at Paspa. I highly recommend them." This feedback is the result of her company's personal commitment to "relationship management."

Ask People What They Do!

Some of the best business leads I have gotten came from my striking up a conversation with a total stranger, especially someone I might, once upon a time, have thought had no business connection to my company's world. It takes only one huge account arising from such a conversation to make a believer out of you! Start the conversation: say hello and ask what people do. Nine times out of ten, they will ask you what you do, too—and that gives you the opportunity to start talking about your business.

I play basketball with a group at my local gym. One day, I finally got around to chatting with one of the guys I had been playing with for years. I asked him what he did for a living. It turned out he was the CEO of a major company—and, thus, someone I wanted to talk to about a possible working relationship! We'd only ever talked hoops up to that point. So always ask people what they do. Always look for a reason to talk about your business. Always ask people to let you know if there's someone you should be talking to about your business.

Remember: *You are the company!*

CHAPTER 9

Technology: Our Generation's Great Equalizer

"Obstacles are things a person sees when he takes his eyes off his goal."

—E. Joseph Cossman, entrepreneur and author

If you're looking for evidence that today's supercharged information tools have broken down barriers and opened up previously unthinkable opportunities for the present tech-savvy generation of entrepreneurs, look no further than YouTube. According to Steve Chen, cofounder of YouTube:

> It happened in January of 2005. It was up at my place in the City, in San Francisco, and we were having a dinner party, and people had digital cameras there, taking normal digital photos as well as movies, and when we tried to share the photos, we found it very easy to share the photos with one another. But when we tried to share the movies, tried to e-mail them, they just kept getting rejected, bounced back. When we tried to upload it, you know, people have different video types—different software. So we sort of took a look, with all the digital cameras now, and with phones being able to take movies, we saw this was going to be more and more of a problem for other people. And we tried to simplify this process, to make it as easy as possible to share these videos on-line. . . . When we first started, we were just trying to share these clips with one another. And we started meeting, actually it was in Chad [Hurley]'s garage.

This video file-sharing service has not only become a global obsession, it also serves as a welcome example of the breathtaking speed of today's connection-driven economy—and, I think, as a warning of the dangers of making overbroad generalizations about that economy. Negative generalizations about exciting new business opportunities that take advantage of the way people communicate today are still very common, still circulated by naysayers who seem to live in a perpetual state of fear, and are still reliably unreliable.

You can still hear people talk ominously about the late-nineties, early-2000s shakeout now known as the "dot-com bubble" as though it were somehow different from any other bubble in business history, or as though starting a business with a plan that embraces the Internet is, by nature, more dangerous or difficult than starting one with a plan that embraces the use of telephones.

Today's amazing capacity for communication makes extraordinary new things possible for you and your business, and you're in a great position to take advantage of that capacity because you belong to a generation that has grown up with personal technology and is not in the least bit afraid of it. Make the most of that fact! YouTube did.

YouTube started as an idea for sharing video files among friends and co-workers Jawed Karim, Chad Hurley, and Steve Chen (quoted in an interview with Charlie Rose that is now featured on—you guessed it—YouTube). The garage-bound business meetings turned into a new global communications medium, and a new *advertising* medium, with breathtaking speed and with all the confidence and energy of its youthful founders. Take a look at the chronology below, and then consider everything that was identified, developed, and built from an interesting idea into a world-changing business in less than two years.

- January 2005: Karim, Hurley, and Chen chat at a dinner party about the need for software that would make it easier to share video files.

- February 2005: The YouTube.com domain is registered.

- May 2005: The site opens to the public.

- Late 2005: The company secures funding from Sequoia Capital, a strategic choice that follows from management's decisions to maintain its high functionality in the face of explosive growth. (Translation: They didn't want the servers going down while people were flocking to the site in vast numbers to see and share videos, and they chose to sell part of the company to make that happen. Obviously a judgment call that worked out well.)

- June 2006: The site announces that 2.5 billion videos were watched on the site during this month alone.

- August 2006: The *Wall Street Journal* reports that the company is hosting over 6 million videos and boasts over half a million subscribers.

- October 2006: Search engine giant Google completes a deal to acquire the company for $1.65 billion in Google stock.

What does it mean? Let's look at the most obvious lesson first. If your concept is solid, your timing is right, and your commitment to your core idea is unshakeable, you can make big things happen, and make them happen quickly. That remarkable story tells us that if you have a good idea for a business, and if that good idea involves people using today's information tools to connect to what they want to connect to, then there is definitely a place for that kind of business in today's economy.

And let's take that idea a little further. If what you are envisioning as a business idea uses today's information technology to *sim-*

plify a process (as YouTube did), and/or it gives more people *access* to a solution to a common problem (like, say, sharing video files), then you may well be able to launch not just a successful new business but also a brand new global social behavior.

It happens! Before Google came along in 1998, people didn't conduct Internet searches the way they do now. Now, Google is the resource of first resort for many of us about—well, everything we don't know yet. Why? Because Google *simplified a process* and made its solution *accessible* to millions of people.

The Broader Implications

Now let's move beyond the question of the business idea itself and look at some of the practical implications of a phenomenon like YouTube. As you read these words, a massive marketing revolution is playing out on the site that Chen and his friends launched from a garage. YouTube's slogan is "Broadcast Yourself," and that's exactly what business owners are doing with it. Type in "sales training," and close to 2,600 videos pop up, most of them connected to a specific sales training company or sales training expert.

Ten years ago, the possibility of a company reaching a global audience more or less instantly with a low-cost video, and securing customers through such videos, would have been fantasy. Now it is a powerful business reality, not just for sales trainers, of course, but also for creators of desktop publishing software, catering and event-planning consultants, and hundreds of other categories of entrepreneurs who have used YouTube to send targeted messages to specific groups of prospects.

As with any other communications medium available to your business—free or paid—the message has to be crafted carefully, the resources invested wisely, and the potential and actual payoff evaluated closely. So, let's look at those requirements.

Effective Communications

How do your prospects and customers communicate and connect with others? My point is not that you should post a video about your company on YouTube. It is that your customers are, right now, probably communicating and connecting in ways that you couldn't possibly have imagined two years ago. If you want to sell to them, find out what they're doing.

Obviously, it's a good idea to use the same communications media your prospects and customers are using right now and keep up on what they will use tomorrow. Monitor what new Web sites they are frequenting, what blogs they are reading, what e-newsletters they subscribe to. Because if you *don't* keep up-to-date on the ways your customers are communicating and consuming the various forms of "new media" that are out there—if you don't find a way to build those media into your own marketing plan—you shouldn't be surprised when your competition does.

REALITY CHECK

Why do you have to keep up with changes in your customers' or prospects' communication habits? Because life changes quickly, and new patterns emerge that soon feel as though they've been around forever! Consider that in the year 2000:

- YouTube didn't exist.

- Facebook didn't exist.

- Wikipedia didn't exist.

- Flickr didn't exist.

- MySpace didn't exist.

Hang out with your prospects and customers, both in person and online. Join their discussion groups. Find out what they're doing in the virtual world, with their Blackberries, iPods, and any other realm that seems appropriate. Listen and learn all you can about what's going on. By doing this, you can identify powerful new ways to launch and promote your business and to target its message.

Often, the new ideas you come up with involving new media don't require much capital. For instance, if you identify a narrow niche of prospective customers that subscribes to a weekly e-newsletter, how much would it cost you to write a great article for that e-newsletter every month that describes your expertise with those people—and establishes your company as a trusted resource? If the articles are solid, and are targeted to a clearly defined group, with a clearly defined problem or interest, your material will be forwarded from one user to another, and will gain credibility as a result. The net cost? The time it takes you to write the articles!

It's amazing how easy it is for me today to keep in touch with all my clients and get them information about my business, Premiere Corporate Events (formerly TSE Sports and Entertainment). I launched my own blog at tsespeakers.com and I also launched a radio show at voiceamerica.com. This way I can communicate with potential clients, suppliers, and even business partners in an entertaining format. But this type of communication was impossible only a few years ago. Technology has given me a way to grow my business and connect with my clients in ways I could not have dreamt of years ago.

One of the most intriguing marketing phenomena of recent years has been the "viral marketing" trend, which has seen savvy entrepreneurs create stuff that users just can't resist forwarding to prospective users—things like Internet links and videos. Consider that YouTube didn't rely on paid advertising to get its message out to users; it *drew in* millions of users by something that might once have been called word of mouth, but is probably now best described as *positive Internet buzz*. That's the act of people forwarding messages and links to each other that point friends and acquaintances to something interesting they have seen on YouTube.

Here's a prediction: By the time you read these words, there will be some new and exciting way for people to communicate with each other, something that they can forward easily to one another, and something that wasn't in existence when this book went to press. Could they use it to point friends and acquaintances toward *your* business? The only way you can possibly know that is by keeping up with the technology yourself.

Using Those New Resources

The advancements in technology over the past decade offer entrepreneurs some tremendous resources. As I've noted earlier, you have access to an astonishing amount of information. For instance, you can research competitors via published legal documents, press releases, and financial reports. Indeed, information on competitors is everywhere on the Web, starting with the companies' own Web sites. With a click of a button you can access this information. What an advantage!

Likewise, you can get the right people to your site. I spoke in Chapter 7 about the importance of creating the right Web site for your business. Now it's time to consider the best ways to get people to visit that site. One of the ways to do that is to have your site be among the top ones to be listed when people do a search for information.

The greatest advantage I see with the Web is in the area of Search Engine Optimization (SEO). SEO is not an exact science, and already thousands of companies have sprung up that will tell you they can get your site ranked at the top of mega-search engines like Google and Yahoo. Still, you can employ particular methods to build your site with SEO-friendly text and to link it with buying strategies that will help your site's ranking.

First, conduct a search of your own for your product or business and see which sites land at the top of the page. Check out those Web sites and see if they list the company that built or promoted their sites. If they do, consider hiring them to help you with your own site. These companies understand title tags, internal links, external links, and all the other factors that go into boosting a site high up on the search list.

These Web site builders also understand the balance you need between site design—how nice your site will look—and actual ranking design. Sites that are built to rank high often have to forgo some design elements, since key words play a large part in SEO. Also, the more key words you have in your site, the better the search engines can find you. Ideally, designers build these keywords into the overall look of the site. Diane Stredicke, who was in the design game at the dawn of the World Wide Web, is a great Web designer who understands SEO and developed one of my first sites. The first thing she will tell you is that you are not going to be able to have the most beautiful site and be able to include every design element if you want good rankings. If there's a conflict between great design and great keywords, go for the keywords.

At present, Google's Adwords program is the 500-pound gorilla for search sponsorship, but other engines like Yahoo and Ask.com are relevant if you get into the pay game. When you are just starting a business, the smarter investment may be to get "naturally" ranked without paying for search-engine sponsorship programs. View your Web site as a work in progress, with one of your tasks being to promote it. And in the future, changes in your business's direction or marketing strategies will mean changes not only in the design but also in the keywords in your Web site.

Once you build a site that is SEO friendly, you can literally put your product in front of the world. Consider that statement carefully! Just ten years ago, it was practically impossible for most businesses to attract attention from global customers. Now people everywhere in the world can view your offerings via the Web, and companies like YouTube make it easy for them to see your videos, too! (Google can even translate your Web site's written content for people who don't speak English.)

Of course, the technology we're talking about here has local as well as global impacts. Whether your clients come from across town or around the globe, you have to say something important about your business that's relevant to their world. A chiropractor in California made a very simple video, using a small portable videocamera, of himself performing a chiropractic procedure on a patient, and he chose keywords that were designed to point searches toward his video. He started getting calls from local prospects who told him that if he was tech-savvy enough to post a video on his Web site, he probably was up-to-date on other aspects of his practice as well!

Of course, technological savvy can have other results in addition to attracting customers. Our organization recently acquired a company called Premiere Sports Travel, based in North Carolina. The company put together experiences, as we did, but they mainly served individuals, not corporations as we were doing. Early on, when many Internet strategies for businesses consisted of simply posting a Web site, Premiere was already working on strategies for SEO. That's one of the elements that convinced us we should acquire the company. Today, when you do a Google search for sports trips or sports packages, Premiere almost always will be the first or second listing. They built their business via the Web because they learned to master the art of SEO.

The Technology Gap

There's another important point about technology that I want to share. Not everyone is going to be as comfortable dealing with technology as you are. It's very likely that some of your important business contacts—including prospects and customers—will be significantly older than you are. That means they will not have grown up with technology as you have and will not use the same communications tools that you do.

This can be a real challenge for some young entrepreneurs. They forget that some people still consider e-mail to be a fairly new—and unwelcome—innovation. For a lot of people, e-mailing is second nature, just as valid a form of reaching out as meeting face to face or calling someone on the phone. They may even consider e-mail their primary business communication tool. But a fair number of people born before 1975 or so were (and may still be) highly resistant to e-mail (or text messaging, or blogging, or Skype, or basically anything other than a personal meeting or a phone call) as a means of conducting business. Call them or meet them in person when they make it clear that that's the way they want the relationship to unfold. You'll both be happier.

It's hard to believe, but there was a time, not so long ago, that computers were *not* part of the typical office environment, a time when cell phones didn't exist, that fax machines were unheard of, and that a "hard drive" was a rough commute home that involved fighting a lot of traffic. As someone who is young and understands technology, you are in a terrific position to benefit from media and information tools that have just emerged—as long as you bear in mind that not everyone is going to be as familiar with the expanded capacity of communications technology as you are.

The *purpose* of all that technology? Delivering great service, of course. To learn about mastering that neglected art, read on.

CHAPTER 10

Service Is What You're Selling

"Our mission 'to be of great service to others,' even with the knowledge that life is full of problems and conflicts, struggle and challenges. Life is one damn thing after another, but I will do everything to make it work because this is our dream. And dreams die last.**"**

—**Scott Mesh, Executive Director, Los Ninos Services**

I've said it elsewhere, and I'll say it again. At some point during your first year of operation you will realize—not just at an intellectual level but also as part of your emotional and physical makeup—that your business is really about *relationships*. That realization must support your organization's service philosophy.

If your business makes it that first year—and since you've made it this far in this book, I believe it will—there is one big reason you can point to when people ask how you did it. At the end of your first year, your business will still be going because you and your partner have discovered, and programmed into your central nervous systems, the central, inspiring reality of entrepreneurship: The service you deliver to support your critical business relationships is your true and only product.

Premiere Corporate Events (formerly TSE Sports and Entertainment) sells experiences. We deliver to our clients unique experiences, or once-in-a-lifetime trips, to top-level events like the Super Bowl, the Masters, and the World Series. Our clients expect the highest level of service when they put their money down for these memorable experiences, and we do our best to make absolutely sure they get that service before, during, and after the event. But the service we deliver is part of the experience we sell. After all, the experience of working with us starts long before people show up at the Super Bowl!

The commitment to ongoing service—the commitment to making sure your customers are happy, no matter what—is the most important thing you are selling. That commitment is what closes deals in the first place. It's what keeps your most important business relationships going and what keeps your customers coming back for more. It's what helps you spot difficult problems, bounce back, and repair the relationship when there is a problem. And it's what gets you happy clients to refer others to you. If the service you deliver is lousy, none of those things will happen!

What Is Service?

Service is more than just putting your hand out for a handshake. It's making sure your customer will shake hands again, and will introduce you to other people to shake hands with.

Service is followthrough. It's remembering to call and check in. It's anticipating challenges before they happen, and calling after so-called business hours to talk about your plans for responding when things go wrong unexpectedly—which they will. It's keeping clients and prospective clients in the loop. It's rewarding employees who do a great job of dealing directly with customers. It's rewarding vendors who do a great job of dealing directly with your customers. It's harnessing your own company's energy and drive—and your own energy and drive—to overcome all the preconceptions, problems, and potholes you will encounter along the way.

Service is giving a damn in a world where most people don't. It's delivering on the promises you make, no matter what. Clients remember that kind of thing. Service is promising to add value, setting expectations based on that value, and then caring enough about the relationship to make sure that the client feels that the expectations have been met. Then, once you have a happy client to call, service is calling that client to check in, even though you have other things to do, for the sake of the relationship.

Much of the repeat business we do with important clients—and a huge number of the referrals we generate—comes from one-on-one phone calls, placed by me and members of my sales team, that have on the surface nothing to do with "business." But these calls have everything to do with respecting and supporting the relationship we've built with a decision maker. That's the ultimate expression of service: checking in to see what's up in the person's world. Those are the kinds of calls I term "relationship calls," the "what's up with you these days?" calls.

A Culture of Adding Value

If you deliver service wisely, if you build a culture of service into your business, you will find that the positive impact of service spreads in all directions, touching everyone and creating connections that last for years, decades, or even a lifetime. Service is delivering value through relationships, and doing that over the long term, not just at the moment you close the deal.

Your company will thrive if the service you provide is top-drawer and if you make a personal commitment to using that service to deliver value to every critical relationship your company initiates. Yes, that's probably an impossible goal. You need to shoot for it anyway, and recommit yourself and your company to it every day. Your company won't thrive if you don't make that kind of commitment.

"The key to creating wealth is simple. It is called 'adding value.' Successful people are those who are always looking for ways to add value in some way to a person, a company, a product, or a service."

—Peter Drucker, writer and management consultant

Clients Come First

You know the old saying: "The customer is always right." Even if you think it's a cliché, even if you have convinced yourself that it's not really true, you must build your business around this idea if you want it to thrive.

I have been in many situations where, deep down, I know my company was not at fault or even the least bit responsible for a problem. It doesn't matter. You must do all you can to rectify a situation when a client is upset. Forget about who's "right." Period.

You must constantly be thinking about the customer, about how to keep the customer happy. As Ken Blanchard, Jim Ballard, and Fred Finch say in their book *Customer Mania! It's Never Too Late to Build a Customer-Based-Focused Company*, "Why is customer focus so important? Because whether you're selling pizzas or professional services, your business is not about you. It's about the people you serve."

But what does pleasing the client mean in actual practice? Let me give you an example from my own experience.

There was an event we set up for a corporate client that involved having an NFL player from the San Diego Chargers show up for an appearance at the Pro Bowl to meet the people this client was hosting. Even though the athlete we arranged to appear was a Pro Bowl player, there was a problem when the client saw his name. Our client believed that this player was not well known enough and that the people who came to the event would be upset when they learned who they'd be meeting.

Here's what I want you to notice: that client's problem was not really a "client problem." It was *my* problem. Personally, I thought the client's group would have been absolutely ecstatic to meet the player. And, of course, if I'd wanted to, I could have started pointing to the "letter of the law." After all, we had promised a Pro Bowl player, and we had delivered on our end of the agreement.

But once you and your client get into discussing the "letter of the law," the relationship is in trouble—or maybe even over. When it comes right down to it, you're not really concerned about who's right and wrong, are you? No. You're concerned about *what it takes to make this client happy*. Who was right and who was wrong no longer matter. All that actually matters is that the customer is happy with the outcome.

What was I supposed to do? My client perceived that he was not getting what he was supposed to receive. So I had to start thinking like he was thinking. I made a last-minute call and arranged for prospective Hall of Famer Lorenzo Neal, who was also a Pro Bowl player, to show up as well. My company picked up the expense and lost money on the deal, but our client was happy and that's what counted. In the end, we added value and protected the relationship. That client knew other potential clients, and when he talked to them, I wanted him to say, "We used TSE and, boy, did they deliver for me!" And he did!

So, put aside any doubts you have about whether the customer is correct, or any inclination you may have to engage in a debate with your customer. These doubts and debates can never be your starting point in the relationship. Yes, with a totally irrational client there does come a point when you should stand your ground. But those cases are very rare. In the vast majority of situations, it is much better to appease than oppose.

You simply cannot afford to have people speaking negatively about your business.

Take Care of the Relationship and the Money Will Follow

If you handle situations and make decisions with the client's interests in mind, first and foremost, your company will always gain more business in the long run. It's important to look beyond an apparent initial loss and realize that, when you make a customer happy, you are giving up a one-time loss for a long-term gain.

Your business really will grow *if* you build, and demonstrate to all of your employees, your company's commitment to putting clients first. As Vincent D'Agostino, president and founding partner of Web loyalty.com, says:

> Customer-service culture starts with the CEO, and should be encouraged throughout the organization. In this culture, the customer is the core of all managerial, financial, and operational decisions. Management consistently demonstrates its customer commitment to all employees. . . . Be respectful of time. Prompt responses to telephone calls and e-mails show respect. Review internal processes and remove roadblocks and delays. Publicly reward customer-service heroes. Consider the lifetime value of your customers. Get it right, right away. Satisfaction levels drop each time a customer has to follow up on a request or an issue. Try to thoroughly and accurately address customer queries—the first time.

Following the "customer first" principle is mandatory. And if it doesn't start with you, who is it going to start with? Whether you have a computer repair company, sell shoes at retail, or send Fortune 100 sales teams to the Super Bowl as a sign of appreciation from top management, your guiding business idea is going to be to make sure your customer is happy.

You must find a way to deliver great service. The computer user is complaining that the computer you fixed still isn't working properly? You must try to find a way to make him happy. The customer says the dress shoes she bought from you are falling apart after two days of wear? You must try to find a way to make her happy.

*"*You'll never have a product or price advantage again. They can be easily duplicated, but a strong customer service culture can't be copied.*"*
—Jerry Fritz, leading customer service speaker and trainer, and founder of THE POWER TO WOW

Tell Them the Truth, Tell Them Your Plan

One important component of service is that of being straightforward with your customers. They want to know that the company they are working with is looking out for their interests at all times. That means being upfront about everything of consequence that affects them.

Sometimes the news you have to deliver will not be positive. Any reasonable client understands that things will go wrong from time to time. What the customer needs to feel is that you are on top of the problem. A lot of companies, for example, make the mistake of holding back bad news and trying to bury problems when they arise. They are afraid the client will react negatively, so they don't deliver the bad news until the last possible moment. This kills relationships.

"Customers don't expect you to be perfect. They do expect you to fix things when they go wrong."
—Donald Porter, British Airways executive

The way you approach problems and how you handle them will determine how comfortable a client will feel working with you. The moment a problem arises is the moment to show a customer what you're made of. Clients want to be dealt with honestly and be apprised of situations at all times so they can feel in control. Some of my best client relationships have developed out of "problems" that came up. We looked for ways to turn those problems into opportunities.

Every problem or challenge you face in a customer relationship is an opportunity to show the client you can be trusted and can rectify the situation. In many cases, if you simply show the clients you care about their situation, that is sufficient for the clients to feel comfortable working with you. So, look at any bad situation as a way to communicate and improve the relationship. If you skip the communication part, you will only be undermining—and perhaps even destroying—your connection with the customer.

Think of a commitment to superior service and superior relationships as your company's insurance policy against those inevitable delays, disappointments, and, yes, disasters that are going to occur as you carry out parts of your business plan. Since many—probably most—of your competitors will not have the commitment to service that you will have, you can turn this commitment into a secret weapon and a major competitive advantage.

Saving Room for Dessert

Pete Morolla, who owns several high-end bakery shops in New Jersey, operates a big catering business for large corporate events. He contracted with my company to deliver ice cream and desserts for a 500-person luncheon we were organizing for a major corporate client. Very early on the morning of the event I received a call from Pete. His delivery truck had broken down en route to New York City. That meant all his great desserts were sitting somewhere in a breakdown lane on the New Jersey Turnpike.

Pete apologized for calling so early, and told me he didn't want to bother me, but that he wanted me to know he was working on a solution to the problem and to make me aware of the potential for delay. The fact that he chose to call, rather than to "bury" the bad news, showed that he respected me and our relationship enough to tell me the truth about a bad situation. Notice, too, that Pete didn't hide behind the excuse of waiting until "normal business hours" to reach me. He knew I was up, and he knew that I would want to know what was going on.

Many of Pete's competitors would never have picked up the phone at that hour and admitted they were having a problem, but Pete always makes a point of being straightforward and honest with me. He told me he was going to send another truck from his other shop that would pick up the food and deliver it as soon as possible. I now knew what was going on. I had all the information Pete had about what was likely to affect my event. Pete soon called me back to let me know the transfer had been made and the food would arrive—about an hour later than he had expected. This was not an ideal situation, of course, but it was much better knowing what was going on than not knowing. I had to decide what to do next. Because we knew the desserts were now en route, we started the event on time and, as it turned out, dessert was actually served on time.

Of course, I wasn't thrilled when I heard about Pete's problem, but I understood that trucks do break down unexpectedly. It was comforting to have Pete call and let me know he was on top of the situation, and was doing all he could to make it better. As a result of his accountability Pete has forged a strong relationship with my company.

Here's my question for you: What would have happened if he hadn't called, and had simply delivered the desserts late? It's amazing how many people would hesitate to call a client when a problem like this comes up. By reaching out to me Pete was able to turn a negative into a positive. You must use the same approach to turn problems into improved relationships with your clients.

A Tale of Two Tailors

I know the owner of a clothing shop that sells custom men's suits. I was always surprised that his store was packed, even though his prices were considerably higher than his competition across the street.

I needed a suit on short notice for a conference that I was attending. I asked the owner if he could rush the order and still get me the same quality suit in time for the conference. He was honest and told me he definitely would not be able to deliver the same quality in that short a period of time. He said he did not want to jeopardize the situation by telling me he could get it done. I couldn't understand why he couldn't make it happen for me. I decided to take my business across the street. The shop owner on the other side of the avenue guaranteed me that he could have a custom suit for me in time for the conference. He was very reassuring, so I decided to purchase the suit from him and not worry about anything. As the day of the conference got closer I got more and more nervous, especially after I was told the suit was being held up in customs and it was out of his hands. The shop owner still assured me it would be delivered in time and not to worry. The conference came and went, and it wasn't until two weeks later that I received my suit. It didn't even fit me correctly.

Honesty, realism, and trustworthiness are the reasons the first tailor's shop is always packed, despite those high prices. And I think the lack of honesty may have something to do with the fact that the other shop owner went out of business a few months after my disastrous experience with him.

Seeing the Truth

The above two examples of service quality reflect my experiences. Here's a story of someone else who faced disappointment, this time posted on the Internet for all to read:

> I showed up on Saturday to pick up my glasses, which were supposed to be ready on Friday. They told me that the delivery didn't come and to come back on Monday. Naturally, when I called on Monday,

I was told that they were not yet ready, but I should call end of day on Tuesday, and the owner would personally deliver and fit my glasses. She even gave me her cell phone number. On Tuesday, I left a message on her cell phone and never did receive a call back— Tuesday, Wednesday, Thursday—I left messages that were not returned, and it became obvious that my order had not been placed, or that something had gone horribly wrong. Throughout all of this, I received no call from the owner and on Friday my glasses were delivered, by an assistant—with no professional fitting. Will I go back there? Will I recommend them? What I know is that everyone involved overpromised and then clearly underdelivered. There is no quicker and surer way to destroy your reputation.

Have you noticed how everyone—including you—has a horror story from the world of customer service that sounds more or less like the one above? Have you noticed how rare it is that those stories turn around and end happily for the customer?

Problems happen. We all know that. But the businesses that really separate themselves from the pack find ways to turn *potential* customer service disasters into shining success stories by taking action quickly, taking ownership of the problem, and then keeping on the same track until the customer is happy.

That kind of turnaround is *not* what happened in the eyeglasses story above, but it *is* what happened not long ago when Amazon.com messed up an order I'd placed. I was supposed to receive a book within 24 hours, and it didn't arrive. I sent an e-mail via the Amazon.com site's customer service section, and within hours I received a personalized e-mail and a promise that the book would arrive the next day by overnight courier. It did!

According to Jeff Bezos, founder of Amazon.com, "We see our customers as invited guests to a party, and we are the hosts. It's our job every day to make every important aspect of the customer experience a little bit better. . . . If you make customers unhappy in the physical world, they might each tell 6 friends. If you make customers unhappy on the Internet, they can each tell 6,000 friends."

Keep Paying Attention

Most clients need to know that you are thinking about their business as much as they are. If they don't hear from you on a regular basis, no matter how much time and effort you are putting in on their behalf, they are going to assume that you have stopped thinking about them and stopped working for them. And who can blame them? Don't you assume someone has stopped thinking about you when that person drops off the radar screen?

Keep in touch with your clients on a regular basis by reporting in with updates on their projects. Stay in contact on a weekly basis, no matter how much or how little there really is to report. Consistent communication will only strengthen your relationship. Some clients will tell you that they don't need to hear from you all the time. Stay in touch anyway. Whether they realize it or not, staying in touch and supporting the relationship is what they are paying you to do. If they don't hear from you, they will eventually turn to someone else who *does* check in with them more often.

As Solomon Robert says in his book *The Art of Client Service*, "Once a client, always a client." I would add a footnote to that: Once a client, always a client—*if* you continue to service your client *continually*, not just when it's time for them to re-up on a contract. If you fall into the pattern of ignoring clients until it's time for them to renew with you, you will risk losing them altogether, even if you have been doing a great job!

> *"*Being on par in terms of price and quality only gets you into the game. Service wins the game.*"*
> **—Tony Alessandra**

Years ago, I had a major client I felt I was doing great work for. I didn't try to keep in touch with him because I knew he didn't want to be bothered. I figured that if he needed something, he would call me and I would take care of it for him. In my mind, we had developed a great relationship. I assumed that I was his go-to contact for all of his sports travel programs. I'd done a great job for him, hadn't I?

While I sat back and let things linger, he was getting calls from all of my competitors. Sure enough, he accepted an invitation to play golf with one of those companies. And soon enough I was splitting his business with a rival. Shortly thereafter, I lost his business altogether. Why? Because my competitor had been willing to put in the time and call him for maybe ten minutes, once a week, and took him out to lunch once a month!

Servicing the client, supporting the relationship, thinking like the client have to be your number one priority in your business. This idea will come up again and again in this book, but I've devoted a whole chapter to it here to stress its importance. If you want your new business to make it past the one-year mark, you must make your client relationships your primary concern—the concern you always come back to at the end of every long day and the beginning of every new one.

In the next chapter, you'll see how this idea of service carries forward to finding ways to *overdeliver* on what you promise. This is one of the great—and underused—principles for long-term success in business.

"A lot of people think that the new economy is all about the Internet. I think that it's being fueled by the Internet—as well as by cell phones, digital assistants, and the like—but that it's really about customers.**"**
—Patricia Seybold, leading customer service consultant, and founder of the Patricia Seybold Group

CHAPTER 11

Back Up Your Sell

"A sale is not something you pursue; it is something that happens to you while you are immersed in serving your customer.**"**

—Anonymous

Have you noticed how people like to crack jokes about opportunistic, vaguely dishonorable salespeople? Have you thought about the stereotypical salesperson—fast talker, focused on short-term gain, not particularly trustworthy? Why do you think this stereotype is so common? Salespeople—and companies—who focus on the front end of the sales relationship earn, and deserve, this stereotype.

Anyone can win a piece of business by paying a lot of attention to the front end of a sale, and indeed many salespeople will promise anything to get that deal done. But this practice can be dangerous to your business, especially if you know that you cannot deliver on the promise you have made.

How to Lose a Client

You will never get a client to return if you do not back up your sale. That means nothing more than servicing your customer in exactly the way you made the sale. To do this, you build a habit in your company of *selling light and performing heavy*. You'll hear other people express this principle as underpromise and overdeliver, but I think *selling light and performing heavy* is a better way to describe what happens. I don't want to start any client relationship by "underpromising"; maybe I don't like the way that word rattles around in my head. It sounds like I'm making an excuse beforehand for something that will not come later.

Selling light and performing heavy keeps clients happy and working with you over the long haul. It means making clients *more* important after you close the sale, not less important. So many entrepreneurs put huge amounts of time into acquiring new business and not enough time into servicing their existing business. If you don't take care of the business you have brought in the front door, you will lose it right out the back door.

I wasn't a big fan of Bill Walton, the professional basketball player, when I was growing up, but that was only because he played for the Boston Celtics and I was a big New York Knicks fan. I will tell you I am a huge supporter of his nowadays. Bill has his own brand now, and he has built a business around Bill Walton the Celebrity.

Walton has many speaking engagements, for which he receives an appearance fee. Like most paid speakers, Bill charges a minimum two-hour fee for each appearance. This is standard in the industry. Most speakers are clock-watchers and they make sure they don't spend even a few extra seconds of time with a client if they are not being compensated for those seconds. That's not how Bill does business, though. In fact, on many occasions he has stayed until the last person in the audience has left the building or doesn't want to listen to him talk anymore. Believe me, this is virtually unheard of!

Walton really cares about his performance, and he cares about making sure the client is satisfied. His contracts with clients spell out all of his obligations, and he never promises more than he has agreed to upfront. And yet everyone who has done business with Bill says the same thing: "He overdelivered on what we expected from him."

Since Bill Walton is known for this behavior in the market, his reputation has gotten him a lot more business than other speakers in the same field. I would not be at all surprised to learn that Walton's habit of "backing up his sell" has something to do with his coach at UCLA, the legendary John Wooden. Wooden's driving principle was a commitment to personal excellence and to delivering the best possible performance "on the court," whether that be in a basketball game or in the larger game of life. Walton was one of John Wooden's most prominent students, and Walton's success as a broadcaster and speaker after a stellar sports career is a tribute to his mentor's quest for excellence and his habit of coaching the whole person, not just the athlete.

> **"**Here is a simple but powerful rule—always give people more than what they expect to get.**"**
> **—Nelson Boswell, British journalist and biographer**

What Are You "Guaranteeing"?

One of my favorite examples of backing up the sell is Eric Hoffman. Eric is a young entrepreneur who runs a telecommunications company called M5 Networks. His company provides Internet phone service for corporations as an alternative to some of the old-school players like AT&T and Sprint. One client of mine that used M5 Networks commented on how much money the company was saving on its phone bills as a result. I was intrigued and asked Eric to make a presentation to our company. I pressed him about the savings my client was getting and asked him to guarantee those savings for us. He told me he couldn't guarantee the same savings, but he assured me my costs would be less than what I was paying at the time.

In the end, we made the change to M5 Networks. Soon enough I realized I wasn't only paying less than before M5 Networks came on board, but I was actually saving *more* than my client had told me was his experience. So, M5 Networks had performed heavy. I now recommend them to other businesses looking for good service and cost savings from a telecom provider.

You see, in business honesty is the *only* policy. If you are honest, you will be able to grow your business and develop relationships that last a long time. That's because most people prefer to deal with others who have integrity and who engage in above-board business practices. Most people only buy from someone they trust. This behavior comes down to credibility, and it is essential for successful business relationships.

How often do you hear business pundits offering ways to "build credibility" or "establish credibility" with a prospect, including elaborate theories on the best ways to do this? There is only one way to build credibility, and that is to tell the truth to clients and prospective clients, and then to perform heavy. I learned long ago that if you don't give your clients exactly what you tell them you will give them, that lie will come back to haunt you in the end. And, yes, sometimes that means taking a loss.

Give Your Word . . . and Make It Count

My friend Jack owns a premium product supply company, and he once made a terrible mistake that could have cost his client thousands of dollars. He had said he would be able to deliver handmade bags from China for a sales conference by a certain date. When the bags were held up by the Chinese customs people a week before the event, he knew he was not going to be able to deliver the bags on the date he had promised, because the paperwork would not be completed by that point. He did not wait. He took action. He let his client know ahead of time that this problem had occurred. Without hesitating, he went out and purchased the same product at twice the expense in the United States—to make sure he kept to his word. He ended up losing a lot of money on the deal, but he kept the client happy.

Perhaps you're wondering: what was the reward for his honest business practices? Because Jack was true to his word, the client re-booked right after that for another large order for another event!

The Big Lesson

I cannot say it too often: Servicing the client is your number-one priority in business. Whether you are a start-up business or in charge of a Fortune 500 company, keeping the client happy must always be at the top of your list. Over the years I have heard many great business minds make different statements about service, but they all translate to the same thing: Take care of the client or someone else will.

In the last couple of chapters I have stressed the need to communicate constantly with your clients and be completely honest with them. Particularly, if you are young you will most likely need to prove yourself by meeting a certain level of service before clients will trust you. Keep pushing, keep meeting people, keep making your case, keep giving your word about what you *know* you can deliver. If you are making it clear that you are realistic, that you are committed to the truth about what you can and can't do for a client, and that your word is your bond, you will find clients willing to consider giving you a shot.

> *"You have to perform at a consistently higher level than others. That's the mark of a true professional. Professionalism has nothing to do with getting paid for your services."*
> **—Joe Paterno, legendary college football coach**

Once you find those clients, sell light and perform heavy. You'll outshine the competition, win repeat business, and build a powerful reputation for your business. You may be a professional, under Paterno's definition, but what about everyone else in your organization? To learn about assembling and motivating the perfect team, turn to the next chapter.

CHAPTER 12

Inside Players: Your Team

*"*The ratio of We's to I's is the best indicator of the development of a team.*"*

—Lewis B. Ergen, author and motivational expert

Entrepreneurship—real entrepreneurship—means moving beyond the stage where you as the founder are delivering all or most of the good results yourself. Entrepreneurship, in any meaningful sense of the word, means building a good team.

It is surprising how many people who want to start a business are actually uncomfortable with the idea of hiring others and find ways to avoid dealing with the essential step of delegating work. For instance, plenty of people launch small consulting practices or service firms that are built around an individual's expertise, and though they may not admit it out loud, they want to keep the business small. They don't have a plan for building the team, and they never make it a priority to track down good people who could be just as talented as they are at doing what they do. They never find a way to make someone else the point of contact for customers or prospects. Instead, they look for ways to handle every sales opportunity and customer problem themselves—and they still think of themselves as entrepreneurs!

Technically, perhaps they *are* entrepreneurs, but they are not people who are interested in growing a company. I think anyone who builds a permanently small-scale business is missing out on the fun of launching a business idea. The whole point is to grow the company, and the big payoff is in recruiting, training, and retaining the inside players who will take your company to the next level.

Caution: If you think you alone can take your company to the next level of its growth, you're wrong! Your business won't grow much if it is "all you." You have to learn to let go and let others succeed, too. I realized early on that I would have to hand over the big accounts I had brought in to other salespeople. This move was necessary if I wanted these people to grow professionally and be confident enough to go out and get their own clients for me.

Delegating work and developing your employees' skills is sound business strategy. Once you have begun to build an elite team, that team can start turning your vision into reality, but you have to begin delegating important responsibilities to these people and refining the processes they will use to deliver great results themselves. Once you have begun coaching them yourself or have found someone who can coach them for you, then you will know for sure that you are building your company, and not just maintaining a one-person or two-person show. Indeed, one of life's great lessons comes when the company founder figures out how and when to step back and allow others to do the things he or she used to do. If you avoid learning that lesson, your company will suffer.

Pepsi-Cola was one of the first major clients I was able to bring on board at my company. I worked extremely hard to land the account, and I was able to grow the business to a certain degree because of it and I established strong relationships with the firm. As the company grew, and I had more and more responsibilities, I knew I couldn't possibly service Pepsi Cola the way I had early on. I also knew that I had to jump-start a lot of the young salespeople I had brought into the organization and they needed to see some personal success.

Likewise, I wanted to grow the company to the point at which my partner and I could sell the business for millions of dollars. I knew no one would buy us if I were the only person bringing in the big accounts! I gave the Pepsi Cola account to one of these young salespeople. I also handed off some of my other bigger clients, like Frito-

Lay and Anheuser-Busch. It was not easy emotionally, at least at first. But it worked. My sales team gained confidence, and over the years the accounts grew to even bigger levels.

Building a Great Team

There is a time to delegate and a time not to delegate, and when you're just getting the company off the ground, it's likely you do most of the work yourself. In fact, it's quite common for companies to go through a period early on when the founder (or founders) do all the leg work and shake the hands of every customer.

For instance, two guys named Ben and Jerry started selling ice cream in Burlington, Vermont, back in the late 1970s. They really did scoop a lot of ice cream themselves, by hand, and they really did make a lot of deliveries to local stores from the back of a battered Volkswagen. But that was in the early days of their business. Eventually they decided, like all great entrepreneurs, to step back, think more about values, systems and processes, and relationships, and start building and supporting the team that would be capable of taking their business to the next level.

The Ben and Jerry's example is a particularly powerful one. Even though Ben Cohen and Jerry Greenfield no longer own or operate the company, they brought their spirit to the task of assembling not just any team but the right team. They built a team of "inside players" for Ben & Jerry's—people fully committed to the business, who could serve as real allies, not short-term hires.

Shared Values

Ben and Jerry built their great team by being clear about the values that drove the company. The founders wanted everyone they even considered hiring to know that they were auditioning for a special kind of business. The company's mission was driven by a certain set of values—values that said, explicitly, that profit making and social activism go hand in hand, and that the business had an obligation to give something back to society. (That doesn't have to be your message, of course, but it certainly was theirs.) They attracted people who shared those values because they actively recruited for those attitudes. The candidates had to share the founders' vision for the business.

It sounds simple, I know, but the sad fact is that most entrepreneurs don't do this. Think about it. If somebody *doesn't* share your vision for your business, why on earth would you want to hire that person if you didn't have to? So, essential to this step is ascertaining what your values are and how ready you are to talk about them with potential employees.

Rewards for Quality Improvements

Ben and Jerry bought into a concept called Total Quality Management (TQM), which was a system of production management pioneered by (among others) William Edwards Deming, an American business consultant and statistician. Deming's basic idea was (and is) that any time a team has a chance to improve quality in a measurable way, that improvement will ultimately benefit the business's bottom line. Thus, TQM is basically designed to build in awareness of quality at all levels of the organization. (Do a Google search for TQM and learn more about this—you'll be glad you did.) Ben and Jerry hired, trained, promoted, managed, and operated the business with this TQM concept in mind, and thus built a team that wasn't focused solely on processing ice cream, but instead on attaining the highest possible level of quality in all the systems and processes that might possibly relate to ice cream.

To give you just one example, *every* employee on the processing floor at the Ben & Jerry's main plant had the authority, and the responsibility, to make quality-control decisions. "We don't count on quality control to decide . . . what's salable," one manager said, "anyone who comes in contact with the product can make that decision." Similarly, anyone with an idea for improving a system or process had immediate access to top management—that is, Ben or Jerry—and the opportunity to share the idea.

So, how committed are you to quality? And how willing are you to give your team members the authority to make it happen? How are you going to reward them if they do make it happen? And how much access are you going to grant them when they have ideas about new ways to make quality happen?

Strong Relationships

Perhaps more than any other company in its industry, Ben & Jerry's placed a premium on maintaining strong emotional ties with its employees and making sure that they were actually enjoying what they were doing. The founders did this in countless ways. Among the most memorable was the creation of a special committee, known as the Joy Gang, whose sole purpose was to spread fun—that's right, fun—into all corners of the organization. At the time, one of the members of the gang, Sean Greenwood, described it as follows: "Another unique way that we involve individuals is to offer cash 'Joy Grams'—up to $500—to any department that can offer a suggestion on how an event/idea can bring more joy to the workplace. Among ideas suggested and implemented: a hot-chocolate machine for our freezer crew, a gas grill on our patio, and sports equipment for a company softball team." Is it any wonder that a job at Ben & Jerry's became one of the most sought-after occupations in the state of Vermont?

No, you don't have to buy everyone a gas grill as you're trying to get the company off the ground, but be sure you are willing to have a personal connection with every person you hire. How able are you to find ways to build fun into their jobs? How, exactly, are you going to show them that you care for them as people?

Ben & Jerry's didn't just hire employees. In a very real sense, it hired an extended family. That's what Chris Rosica did, as well. According to Rosica, founder and CEO of Rosica Strategic Public Relations, and past president of the Young Entrepreneurs Organization:

We choose our people carefully, and we place a lot of importance on the quality of the relationships we develop, because the right relationships pay off in both the short term and the long term.

Sometimes they pay off in ways that you don't expect. We have had a number of employees who have left the company and gone on to become important allies for our organization. One woman who used to work for us went on to do new things, and eventually became the head of public relations at a private school. She gave us a referral on someone who ended up turning into a client for us, and is still with us today. The lifetime value of that client thus far has been about two hundred thousand dollars.

So, if someone doesn't think of you as something more than a former employer, that person probably isn't going to send a two-hundred-thousand dollar referral your way. But if you're more than just a former employer, referrals may come your way.

Of course, like any business owners, Ben Cohen and Jerry Greenfield made their share of personnel mistakes. But what they accomplished in terms of team creation and teambuilding before they sold the company was extraordinary. Everything they did ultimately connected to their desire to build and grow a certain kind of great company. Once people are truly committed to helping you grow not just any company but a certain kind of company that they believe in—you will find it easy to get them to start treating you, and your company, like family. If you take this approach, employees will respond like family, and you will foster a great working environment.

REALITY CHECK

You will need to treat your employees like family from the very first moment you hire someone. You will need to treat your employees like family no matter how big you grow as an organization. That doesn't mean you will never make a hiring mistake, and it certainly doesn't mean you will never fire anyone. But it does mean that the people you keep on feel that they are part of something larger than themselves, something that is worth making sacrifices for.

Empower the Best, Lose the Rest

"The best leaders are those most interested in surrounding themselves with
assistants and associates smarter than they are. They are frank in admitting
this and are willing to pay for such talents.**"**

—Amos Parrish, American author and advertising executive

I can't express how important it is to hire the right people. Enthusiasm and a positive attitude will do more for your company than any
other attribute in an employee. Of course, you want to hire smart
people who will do a great job, but someone who doesn't have a great
attitude, or who never gets passionate about anything, probably
shouldn't be a member of your "family." You want to look first and
foremost for people who "get" your vision, who are dedicated to putting forth the best of themselves and others, and who are truly motivated. These are the people who will make your company strong.
Look for those qualities first, and then identify who within that group
has the skills you need.

Walt Disney made a habit of hiring recent art college graduates
whose attitudes he liked—and then training them in the deeper skills
he needed in them to develop as animators. I think the results his
studio generated speak for themselves.

By the same token, you will want to keep an eye out for people
with advanced skills who are capable of helping you execute your
business plan—or maybe even bring it to a whole new level. An essential, but often ignored, hiring rule is easy for some entrepreneurs to
overlook: Never, ever be afraid to hire someone who is smarter than
you are or who has skills that you don't have.

I recommend that you make any hiring decision provisional, and that you use the first ninety days (at least) as a test to figure out whether this person really does belong in your community. This is one way a business is a lot better than a real family—you can audition people and get rid of them if they are making your business dysfunctional; not so with blood relatives!

Any smart business person will tell you that employees are what make or break a company. Positive, energetic, and committed employees create a successful environment; unfortunately, negative or lethargic employees can doom your business. I learned this lesson the hard way.

We had an employee named Arnie who was extremely negative and also manipulative. Unfortunately he was also one of my top salespeople. I knew Arnie's attitude was affecting other people in the company, but I was hesitant to let him go because he was bringing in some great accounts. That was a mistake, and it's one that I have not repeated.

Arnie lived to sow dissension in the ranks. His attitude threatened to turn us into a dysfunctional family. I should have done something about that long before I did, but the truth is it took me a while to realize that his great sales record was simply not worth the trouble he was causing. Tensions rose and pressure built before I took action. I regret the delay now, because I was letting the other team members down and morale was at an all-time low. Remember, employees will come and go, but you must never allow a negative employee to become a cancer in your organization. Everyone has a bad day from time to time, but it's up to you as owner of the business to notice what is going on and take action to remedy the situation.

Here's the interesting part. I thought that letting Arnie go was going to hurt our organization's revenues. But exactly the opposite was true. In the weeks after I let Arnie go, morale rose like a sky-rocket. The other salespeople and our internal staff thanked me and said how much of a drain he had been on them. And by six months later our sales had almost doubled! The other sales reps had picked up Arnie's business and were able to achieve even more with his old accounts. Remember, atmosphere and environment are more impor-tant than any one employee.

Give People Credit

"A group becomes a team when each member is sure enough of himself and his contribution to praise the skill of the others."
—Norman Shidle, author and entrepreneur

It is to give team members proper credit when they deserve it. When someone is doing a great job, let the whole company know. Make people winners; never hog the credit for yourself. In fact, even when you may have helped out a little, let your employee enjoy the spot-light.

You will find that some employees love praise even more than financial rewards. Wherever you can honestly do so, give that praise to them. Praise breeds confidence, which creates strong employees. If you are able to praise others publicly for a job that has truly been well done, you will build a loyal workforce. Yet this kind of praise is often hard for some entrepreneurs to offer. If you fall into that category, push your limits a bit and practice giving believable praise.

Of course, you can also encourage employees to praise one another. On a visit to a major client of ours, Hershey Chocolate Company, I noticed in the lobby of the corporate headquarters building a bulletin board. Examining it closer, I saw loads of greeting cards that employees had sent to each other, giving credit for doing something positive for the company. The company had created specific cards for a variety of positive behaviors; employees could then send these cards to other employees so they would feel appreciated. I was impressed that such a large company would do something so small-town as this.

When I got back to my office, I ordered my own set of cards so that employees could send similar positive messages to each other. The program has been a huge success and a great morale booster in the office.

It Starts with You

A final word of advice: You cannot hire or motivate employees who will create a positive work environment at your company. A positive work environment starts at the top, with you.

If you demonstrate, on a regular basis, that you trust people and that you can be trusted, that you understand that mistakes happen and that making mistakes is the only way people learn, that you are committed to bringing optimism and positive energy to the business, you will build a work environment in which employees and managers model those same values. In contrast, if you pick people apart, find only faults, and withhold praise even when it has been earned, your negativity will inevitably lead to a negative work environment.

This is not what some entrepreneurs want to hear, but it is reality. If you do not treat your people well, you cannot build a truly great organization. It is as simple as that. Treat your employees with honesty and respect, lead with faith and integrity, and you will develop a working atmosphere in which people will excel. This atmosphere will be evident to your customers and your turnover will be low. And when people finally do move on, they will remain allies, helping to move your business to the next level.

"Keep away from people who belittle your ambitions. Small people always do
that, but the really great make you feel that you, too, can become great."
—Mark Twain

A business really does take on the personality of its leader. There is simply no escaping that fact. A lot of entrepreneurs are under the impression that they have a staffing or personnel problem, when in fact what they have is a leadership personality problem. I believe that any problem can be overcome, including leadership issues at the top. I also believe, however, that you have to recognize a problem before you can begin to overcome it. That's as true in the area of teambuilding as it is in any other challenge your organization will face. To learn about the art of rewarding your employees, read on.

CHAPTER 13

Celebrate Failure, Reward Success

"You may not realize it when it happens, but a kick in the teeth may be the best thing in the world for you.**"**

—Walt Disney

Failure. Failure is an essential part of the learning curve. Yet, how often we choose to not look at failure in a positive light! In fact, lots of young entrepreneurs see failure as one of the two possible outcomes they can deliver, and as the worst of the two outcomes. It's the outcome that must be avoided at all costs, the one that is associated with pain and trauma. We've been told "failure is not an option."

Yet, as radio commentator and humorist Garrison Keillor points out, "A person who does not know failure is a person with a poor sense of reality." Keillor goes further, warning that someone who goes through his twenties and thirties "racking up one prize after another—the beautiful size-four wife and the starter mansion and the two beautiful, gifted children with the Celtic names . . . is a man who is headed for a gigantic mid-life crisis in which he runs away with a waitress named Misty and perms his hair and becomes a 45-year-old singer/songwriter. You don't want to do that."

Three Important Points About Failure

Consider these three points carefully:

- *Point Number One:* You learn the least when you succeed, and you may actually learn nothing at all when you succeed. For instance, you may believe that closing a big deal was the result of your superior research on the company you chose or your great sales presentation, when in fact the client chose you because another vendor backed out at the last minute and had no choice but to go with you—but didn't tell you this.

- *Point Number Two*: You learn the most when you fail. This is just the way the human nervous system works. When you experience pain and displeasure, you draw conclusions at a deep level about what caused that pain and displeasure, and you may learn some effective strategies that will help you avoid the experience in the future. For instance, losing your only client when that client is bought out by another company is likely to teach you, in a profound and impossible-to-forget way, about the potential cash-flow risks connected with having only one client, even if that client is big.

- *Point Number Three*: A successful business requires that its leaders learn a great deal, and keep on learning over time. You could even define a successful business in terms of its experience base, which is nothing more than the lessons people running the business have learned, usually by means of failure.

Think about these three points the next time you feel you have failed.

Failure and the Learning Curve

Business people who fail to see the positive elements of failure don't get one of the central lessons of leadership. They look at failure as though it were a virus. They are characters in a video game, standing in the middle of the screen. The outcome "Success" is hovering brightly to their right and has one thousand points attached to it. The outcome "Failure" is bobbing ominously on their left and is set in darker hues. It has negative one thousand points attached to it, or maybe even death! The only question they can ask is, "How do I avoid failure and move toward success?"

Failure may not be your favorite option, or even the option you plan for, but there is no reason to demonize it when it occurs. Demonizing failure makes it hard for people in your company—including you—to learn what to do when things don't go as you planned.

What if you were to design another video game? What if you were another character in another setting, and this time you were situated on the far left-hand corner of the video screen? What if, in the middle of the screen next to you, was a cloud labeled "Failure," rather brightly colored this time and bearing a reward of 250 points—if you kept moving forward once you passed through the cloud? (You do have the chance to learn something when you fail, which makes connecting a reward to failure worth considering in your business.) And what if, on the far right-hand side of the screen there were a big bright box labeled "Success" and bearing a reward of 1,000 points? You could then ask another question, "How could I use failure to get to success?"

What if failure were something that happened on the way to success? If failure weren't a sign of a character flaw, or bad luck (whatever that is), or the wrath of the Almighty? What if the only real sin that connected to failure was wallowing in it? What if you got 250 points every time you failed—as long as you kept moving forward? You'd keep moving forward.

Nobody should set out to fail, or even be complacent about failure. At the same time, "not failing" is an unrealistic organizational goal that will only breed resentment and a sick corporate culture.

Maintaining forward momentum after you fail, and sharing what you've learned with those who can benefit from the information, is by contrast a realistic goal. In fact, it's a goal that every successful entrepreneur learns to master, somehow, in a way that matches his or her personal style.

This is a lesson that doesn't come easily to people who are fixated on short-term outcomes, but it becomes second nature to anyone who takes the long-term view and secures creativity, innovation, and adaptability from his or her team. If you doubt this, look closely at the companies you are competing with. Pick out the company with the best and most innovative business approaches, then track down an interview with the CEO or founder of that firm. Time and again, the people at the top of the top businesses reward the act of *failing and learning* from experience. If the person at the top doesn't reward the failing and learning, and only punishes people when they fail, then employees will try to cover up their failures, they won't learn as much as quickly, and they won't innovate.

If you want a work environment in which people never fail, you will get a team of people who never innovate and never ask questions they don't know the answers to. Is that the team you want?

Congratulations—You Lost the Account

There was a successful advertising executive who used to take his entire office out to lunch after they failed to win a big account. Why did he do this? He wanted his employees to know that he knew how hard they had worked, even though they didn't win the business. He also wanted them to know that he valued all they had learned while trying for the account.

The head of that agency would literally celebrate failures and discuss over lunch some ways he thought they might do better next time. He was not going to let a no from a potential client affect the optimism of his company. This attitude allowed his employees to relax and perform better in client pitches.

Failure, in my book, is not the same as losing. This may sound like a strange distinction to make, but hear me out. As far as I'm concerned, a failure—in this case, a no answer from someone you wanted to do business with—only becomes a loss if it convinces you to stop making forward motion. That's the only outcome I can see from failure that results in your organization actually losing something. With the advertising lunches, the head of that agency was making absolutely sure that his team kept on putting one foot in front of the other, despite setbacks. He realized that if he could get the team to focus on what it had learned from the experience, there would continue to be forward motion as the team made better decisions in the future.

Many of my own best business decisions have come as a result of learning about failures or bad decisions I made. Early on in my career, for instance, I had a prospect ask me about a major project—and I got cold feet. I didn't think we could handle it, didn't think we had the internal resources necessary to make it happen. I watched as a competitor with the same limited resources swooped in and got the deal. That competitor figured out a way to make it work, and I failed. I made a personal commitment to never again let doubt determine my decisions. I go for it and know that I can make it all happen—or figure out a way to get it done. That mind-set has led to a whole lot of big deals, yet it grew out of a mistake! Thank goodness for the mistake.

Ashley Ball, media critic and blogger, notes:

> You, my friend, are a Master Tape Engineer. Your reputation as the King of Stick is riding on your latest project. But the adhesive you've come up with is flabby and weak. . . . It couldn't hold two magnets together. You're flummoxed. You have two choices: Mention this intriguing development to your co-workers or keep it quiet to hide your "failure" rather than exposing it to ridicule. If you chose option one, congratulations. You have just invented the central ingredient in Post-it Notes. You chose the second? Oooh, too bad. Your cover-up was so successful, no one knew you'd made any progress at all. And you never did find that super-adhesive.

Call the Next Play

Here's a reality check: You're going to make a mistake.

So what? When that happens, you're going to go back to the huddle. You're going to think about what just happened. You're going to keep an eye out for interesting new opportunities. And you're going to call another play. You're going to make changes as you go along, maybe even calling an audible at the line of scrimmage (to use a football metaphor for on-field improvisation). And you're going to get better.

You have to be willing to put yourself on the line. There are so many people who won't do that, for the simple reason that they're terrified of failure or terrified that someone will say that they were wrong about something. It's okay—everyone fails at some point. For entrepreneurs, the question is, "How do you keep the failure from becoming a loss for your business?" In the end, that's a matter of stepping back up to the line of scrimmage, not really caring if somebody says that something has gone wrong. Yes, you're the one who's responsible. And that's okay. All that means is you get to call the next play, based on what you now know. If you're willing to do that, and you are okay with being responsible, then eventually you will succeed.

But you have to step back up to the line of scrimmage.

In your case, it's not just you who has to bounce back, of course. The members of your company will experience setbacks, too. That's a given. The question is, "How do you want your team members to respond when this happens? Do you want people to freeze up, stop thinking creatively, stop communicating with each other, and start worrying about survival or what the job market is like? Do you want them to fixate on what will happen to them and their families whenever something happens that didn't turn out exactly the way you'd hoped? If that's what you're after, you should find a way to demonize failure and then humiliate, punish, or browbeat every person on your team whenever a goal goes unmet.

Or do you want people to bounce back, start asking better questions about the situation that didn't go quite they way you (or they) had hoped? Do you want them to regroup as a team, share everything they know about what went wrong, identify new opportunities, and plot a strategy for forward movement? If that's the outcome you want, you should find some way to take people out to lunch, congratulate them on a great effort, conduct a blame-free round-table discussion of what did and didn't work this time around, and change procedures for next time.

A company that learns from its mistakes will bounce back and change its procedures. That's a victory. A company that learns from its mistakes will bounce back and finds ways to apply the new information it has just picked up—and often, in so doing, will spot brand-new opportunities. *That's a victory, too!*

Organizational bounceback: the desire to figure out what went wrong and keep digging. This is one of the most important characteristics of successful people—and successful organizations. This is the behavior you want to model for your team. Everyone fails at some point, but the people who keep chugging along are the ones who finally hit their goals. The same is true of companies.

The real difference between success and failure can be a matter of making one more phone call during the sales day. It can be setting up one more meeting that finally leads to the big deal. So many people stop just short of success, never realizing how close they came to realizing their dreams. If you are willing to ask good questions and keep moving forward, and to help the people on your team to do the same thing, you will reach the other side.

REALITY CHECK

If you learn to bounce back and look for opportunity when things go wrong, you will build a company that bounces back and looks for opportunity when things go wrong.

Friday Night at Seven, Making Cold Calls

Very early on in the history of our company, when things looked quite bleak, I had to remind myself that my job was to look for new opportunities, regardless of what else had happened that day. This was not necessarily an easy thing one night, for I had been through a very long, very grim day. It was just me and my partner sharing a small office at this point, and I was still hammering out cold calls on a Friday night at seven o'clock. I had learned that morning that we got stiffed by a supplier for packages we bought for the Baseball All-Star Game that year in Denver, a setback that was going to cost us $25,000—because we could not let our client down. At the time this was a fortune, and for a moment it made me feel like I had taken a punch to the gut. I certainly knew that our bank account was about to take a punch to the gut.

Even on a miserable day like this, though, I remembered that my job was to bounce back. That's why I was still putting my head down and fighting at seven on a Friday night. Luckily, I reached a guy by the name of Mike Valarose, from Reynolds Metals. Mike was working late, too, and he and I instantly bonded over that. Mike said my timing was perfect. He had a big promotion that he needed help on immediately and his agency of record was gone for the weekend. The only reason he gave me a shot was that he was impressed that I was still around on Friday night.

Suddenly, we had a lot better cash-flow picture. It was this bounceback, this extra effort after what I could have written off as a bad day, that opened so many doors for us back in the days when we were building the business. When you get punched in the gut and you find yourself on the floor, that's when you have to be hard-wired to bounce back and start looking for opportunities. You never, ever know what you're going to find.

That's the big lesson for you as the leader—and, by extension, for your team. There's another constituency that's going to have a huge impact on your company's performance: your vendors. You'll learn about the importance of managing and supporting those relationships in the next chapter.

CHAPTER 14

Your Vendor Relationships Matter

*"*Commitment is the daily triumph of integrity over skepticism.*"*

—Anonymous

Your commitments to others must drive your company's critical relationships. As has been said, commitment transforms promises into realities. We've seen the importance of making commitments to your customers, and then delivering on those commitments. We've looked at the commitment to a vision, a set of values, and to quality as the essentials for building a great team. Now it's time to talk about having a demonstrated commitment to your vendors.

Your vendors—those outside players who make it possible for you to deliver on your commitments to your customers—are special relationships that you cultivate. And in the case of vendors particularly, your words speak boldly of your intentions. Vendors are an extension of your team. Just as you pay your employees for their efforts on your behalf, you pay vendors to do a job for you. Having a good relationship with vendors—relationships that are seen by *both* parties as mutually beneficial—is extremely important. You must constantly manage these relationships and ensure that they are working, not only from your point of view but also from the vendor's point of view.

Support the People Who Support You

Vendors are the critical link in your supply chain that will allow you to transform promises into realities for your customers. That means vendors, too, must be supported and kept happy over time, just as employees must be supported. That means investing some time in the relationship and checking in to see what the person's world is like. Just like your world, the vendor's world is constantly changing. Perhaps even more important, vendors must be *chosen* carefully—just as carefully as you have chosen your employees, if not more so.

Think about it. If a single employee bails out on your vision and starts a pattern of sub-par performance, you have a lot of tools at your disposal for fixing the problem before it gets out of hand. Many players in the organization are in a position to notice what's going on, and if worse comes to worst, you can fire the person before a crisis develops. But if a *single* critical vendor decides that working with you is not all that important to his or her long-term plans, and that vendor starts defaulting on quality or service obligations, that could damage or destroy your critical relationships with customers before anyone in your organization realized there was a problem.

Your vendor relationships matter. First, you must nurture, sustain, and service your relationships with the right vendors and, second, you must do this continuously. This obligation to service vendors comes as a surprise to some new entrepreneurs. They wonder, "Why do I have to 'support' my vendors—after all, aren't we the ones paying them? They're there to support me!" These entrepreneurs may also say things like, "If I make a mistake choosing a vendor, what's the big deal? I can always find someone else."

It's tempting to think this way about vendors, especially when you know you have to treat your customers like royalty. Shouldn't your vendors have the same responsibility to treat you that way? Of course, they should. But the truth is that you have to get them aligned with your mission and help them achieve the major goals that connect to that mission. In the real world, you often have to invest in vendor relationships if you expect those vendors to come through with returns on your investment.

If you are skeptical about this, consider how often businesses fail because of poorly selected or poorly maintained vendor relationships.

If you don't exercise caution and intelligence in selecting your vendors, it is easy to end up with one that will let you down. Even if you pick a great ally, don't automatically expect that vendor to buy into your vision or make sacrifices on your behalf of that vision. Without your help, no vendor can realistically be expected to deliver the extent of commitment that you want, that delivers the "daily triumph of integrity over skepticism."

You are placing the future of your business in the hands of the people you select as key vendors. Without your willingness to reach out and help those vendors, without your willingness to service those vendor relationships, you may be putting your company at risk. That may sound like an exaggeration, but consider the following true story.

Trauma in Tampa

The big lesson I learned about the importance of investing time in vendor relationships came about at one of the real turning points for my business. It was a real "gut-check moment" for me and my partner.

Super Bowl XXXV was scheduled to be played in Tampa, Florida, on January 29, 2001. We put together, and started selling, a number of promotional packages built around a single, powerful idea: People could have a great experience in Tampa—something extraordinary for themselves, their partners, or their key business allies—by taking part in a once-in-a-lifetime party that culminated in seats at one of the world's premier sporting events. This championship game would determine the best team in the National Football League for the 2000 season.

Of course, we started selling the package in 2000, before we had any idea which two teams would be going to the game. We went to work early, striking a deal with a prominent vendor for something like 300 Super Bowl tickets. I had done some business with this vendor before, and I was testing the company by using it for a bigger program. I had heard negative things about the vendor, but I went ahead anyway, although I felt a little uneasy about doing so.

At the time I didn't realize how much it would cost me to ignore my instincts. I found all kinds of reasons to justify fast-forwarding past my misgivings. I had chosen a vendor I knew did a lot of business with people in our industry; I had had a couple of good phone calls; and I had a solid agreement on a price that made good business sense for us. Nothing was going to go wrong, I told myself.

On the sales side, things were going great. Our customers booked a record number of trips with us; we sent the vendor a cash down payment for ticket procurement and we signed a contract. The contract, however, never specified a delivery date, which ended up being a critical loophole that rendered the contract virtually meaningless. But at the time I did not realize that. Perhaps more important, the vendor had no regard for a contract; although he put one together, it was just window dressing, considering his ultimate game plan.

When the final week of the NFL playoffs rolled around, New York City was in a frenzy about the Giants. Seemingly against all odds, after having faltered in the middle of the season, the team won five straight games and clinched an Eastern Conference title that had seemed impossible only a month earlier. The team had made the playoffs despite all the second-guessing and naysaying that surrounded them mid-season. It made for a great story—and it also started the biggest crisis in the history of my business. That week, the Giants began their march through the playoffs, and demand from the New York area for tickets I thought I had locked up for my business went through the roof. That wouldn't have been a problem for anyone, of course, if I had been dealing with a responsible vendor who would live up to his word and respect the spirit of his agreement with me. As it turned out, though, that wasn't the vendor I was dealing with.

Fast-forward to the week of the Super Bowl. The Giants had, astonishingly, secured a spot in the big game and would face an equally unlikely opponent, the Baltimore Ravens, a wild-card team that had managed to win all its playoff games on the road and advance to the championship contest. The two cities, and the nation, were riveted on the upcoming contest, which looked to be a great game pitting two underdogs against each other for one of the biggest prizes in all of sports.

I remember thinking to myself that national interest in the game was going to cost people who hadn't already secured their tickets, as we had. And I was right: Super Bowl tickets sold by brokers at $1,200 the week before the Giants got into the game were now selling for $1,700—a huge run-up in price. I knew all about the increased demand, and I was feeling pretty good about myself for having locked up the tickets while the price was still manageable. I was feeling confident upon arrival in Tampa the Thursday before the game. After all, everything had been taken care of. All that was left to do was to connect with my vendor, pass along our check, and pick up our tickets.

I was enjoying a dinner at Burn's Steakhouse in Tampa with our staff. Many of our clients were already in town. Then I got the call from my vendor. I had been phoning him throughout the day to set a meeting place, and he had not called back until evening. The restaurant was noisy, so I stepped outside to talk.

"I can give you six tickets at our contract price," he said. He was "working" on the rest. Remember, I had 300 clients who were already in or en route to Tampa! I felt physically sick as I processed the news.

"Six?" I asked. "Did you say *six* tickets?"

"Six," he answered.

I had ignored my own best instincts in working with this vendor. And now we were about to be screwed by him because of his poor planning. The vendor had simply taken our order, thinking the price would never rise by as much as it did by the time the big game rolled around. After all, the game was being played in Tampa, of all places, and there had been some talk about how this locale was not as glamorous a venue as places like New Orleans or Miami or Pasadena, where the game had been staged in past years. The vendor had put off buying the tickets, assuming the asking price would only drop as game time neared.

When the Giants got into the playoffs, large numbers of Giants fans who were already either spending the winter months in Florida or were willing to do so, started snapping up tickets. Demand surged. The price that the brokers faced started to go up, not down. As a result of the poor decision my vendor had made to wait for a price drop that never came, I now had a disaster in the offing.

I heard from him again on Friday. The only way to get the tickets, the vendor said, was to get him another $300,000—an additional $1,000 per ticket! Notice when I got this information—on the Friday afternoon before the Super Bowl—which left me only a few hours to make the necessary bank transactions if I were going to agree to this (insane) new arrangement!

This vendor had decided to put me between a rock and a hard place. Because the contract was basically meaningless without a delivery date, he could put the screws on our business instead of paying for his own mistake. If I wanted the tickets, I learned, I would have to sign a waiver relinquishing the option of legal action against the vendor. I believe he was expecting we would walk away from the agreement and allow him to give the tickets to other customers he could service at a profit—or sign the waiver and pay the outrageous markup.

If I had serviced this vendor and gotten to know him better before relying on him in such a critical situation, I would have had a better sense of whom I was dealing with. If I had checked the person's references, I could have found out about similar problems he'd had with other clients, and I would simply have moved on to a more reliable vendor. As it stood, I had the choice of telling 294 of my clients that I didn't have tickets for them—or coughing up $300,000, which was just about everything we had in the bank at the time.

My business was now in jeopardy. Not just this trip—the whole company. My partner and I discussed the crisis, and we immediately opted to pull the money out of the bank and deliver what we had promised to our customer. My brother had to go to the bank and take all of our money out, then fly down to Tampa, where he got in at midnight. The bank had to pull money from different branches to make it happen. It was the right call, but it had been a very hard call to make. We never said a word to our clients about what had happened. And we paid our salespeople the commissions they were due.

Looking back, I realize this was one of the best moves I ever made for my business. Yes, we lost money on our biggest event, an event we had worked all year to sell and manage. But we continued to work with the same clients, who brought large amounts of new business to us. And we learned the importance of choosing vendors we could trust over vendors who claim to have the best price. Speaking personally, I learned the importance of listening to my inner voice when it comes to making calls about who will follow through on their commitments.

In the end, you have to create a vendor relationship with a person whom you can trust. Not a logo. Not a Web site. Not a company. A person.

"The only entities which can have responsibilities are people."
—**Milton Friedman, economist**

Honor Thy Vendors

The truth is that there are a lot of lessons to be drawn from that story (which everyone in our organization knows, whether or not they were with us at the time). The one lesson I want to stress here, though, is that big commitments require big relationships. If you've got a big "deliverable" from your vendor, and you're not absolutely sure what kind of person or organization you're dealing with, you're leaving yourself open to a crisis. Look around. Do some digging. Get some references. Find the right people—the people who will make commitments that you (and, by extension, your customers) can trust. Learn from my mistake; don't wait for this kind of problem to happen to you.

Never forget: following through on your commitments to your customers must always come first. I honestly believe that the day I decided to put my customers first in Tampa was the day I defined my business and made its later success possible. The decision was an agonizing one, but it was the right call. I've since learned that the person who put us through that trauma in Tampa is no longer in the business. Not a big surprise.

Another lesson—not entirely relevant to a discussion of vendor relationships, but worthy of mention here—is the victory that comes eventually if you stay focused. The Giants lost that day, but they came back seven years later as the upset winners over the supposedly invincible New England Patriots in Super Bowl XLII. I think of the Giants' comeback as parallel to my own company's march to the top after that traumatizing weekend in Tampa.

A Final Thought

Two of your most important outside vendors are going to be a good accountant and a good lawyer. For most companies staring out, these are outside players, although some businesses may eventually develop talent internally to handle these functions. In the early years, however, your relationships with these two people are going to be extremely important. Choose them carefully, and invest the time to service the relationship.

At first, your lawyer and your accountant are going to be like role players on a basketball team, making appearances only in special situations. But as your company grows they will become your stars. I was lucky enough to find my lawyer, Carl Koerner, early on after hearing him give a speech at a business event. He has helped guide my decisions and kept us safe from liability over the past ten years. Both Carl and my superb accountant, Michael Shekner, were instrumental in helping me negotiate the best terms of the deal when I sold my business. They also worked to set the best possible terms for my new position with the company, and they gave me invaluable expert advice. (This was, after all, the first time I had ever sold a business.) These kinds of outside players can turn into major inside allies for you and your business.

In the next chapter, we look in a little more depth at the challenge of running your business "by the numbers"—with the help of a good accountant, of course.

CHAPTER 15

By the Numbers

*"*Don't just take the first person who comes along.*"*

—**Michael Kahan, founder, Kahan Travel**

The single best piece of advice I can offer you when it comes to managing the numbers side of your business is, unfortunately, going to be impossible for you to follow: Hire someone as brilliant as Andy Robb as your accountant. It's impossible for you to do this because Andy's taken—I've got him. But you *can* find an accountant who will do the same for your business as Andy has done for mine. It just takes some looking and some astute upfront assessment.

Andy was (and is) a close friend who emerged, early on, as one of the most critical allies for our business. I honestly don't think our growth would have been possible without his contributions. To say that he is gifted with numbers and expert in the art of navigating complex tax laws does him a major disservice. You should be on the lookout for someone *like* Andy in the early days of your business— someone who can do the first half of the job by keeping you organized and on top of your expenses and obligations, but who can, at the same time, do the second half of the job by adapting and expanding as the business starts to take off.

It's fairly easy to find someone who can do the first half of that job for you. It takes a bit of digging to find someone who can do the second half. You'll know when you find that kind of accountant because he or she will be deeply interested in the strategic plan you've set up for your business, will ask you lots of questions about that plan, and will want to learn more about it as it changes over time. A good accountant will ask you good questions about where you plan to go and how you plan to get there.

In short, you want someone who is interested in the long-term implications, not just the short-term, of your business decisions. When you find someone like that, and when you're satisfied with the person's ability to keep track of the filing and recording obligations your business faces, you're looking at a major business ally. Most important, find a way to hold on to this ally. This is not a book on accounting or finance, so I'm not going to get into every detail here. But there are a couple of important lessons I picked up from Andy along the way.

Lesson Number 1: Know When to Show a Loss

Your instincts—and maybe your ego—may be to prove that your business really was a good idea, and to do anything and everything in your power to show it turning a profit in year one or year two. You may even be tempted to underreport your expenses so as to prove to someone (yourself? your parents? the government?) that the business is up and running, just like you said it would be.

The truth of the matter is that it's okay to show losses in your business at the beginning. In fact, the more legitimate expenses you can document in the first few years, the better off you're going to be. Of course, I'm not suggesting that you make up expenses you didn't incur. That's illegal. What I am suggesting, though, is that you make the best financial decision for your company, which may not be the easiest emotional decision: to show a loss in the first couple of years.

When I was starting my company, I had a major personal desire to feel that I was making money, so I didn't put in all of my expenses. Andy showed me that I would have been much better off listing every individual expense and taking the loss, because my tax obligation would have been a lot lower as a result. I learned my lesson in year two and followed his advice. So, in the beginning make sure you account for everything and anything that represents a legal expense related to the business—every hotel stay, every flight, every lunch with a client, every cab to meet with a prospect, and so on.

Lesson 2: Get the Right Software

If you're doing the numbers on your own at first (and that's what a lot of entrepreneurs decide to do), don't reinvent the wheel. Pick a good software program that will allow you to keep track of what's going on in your business. Get familiar with that software and use it regularly. If you have a problem getting your head around the software or dread the idea of entering numbers into a computer, delegate this job to someone else and make sure he or she follows through.

This is one area where you're well advised to follow the path blazed by others. Pick a name-brand software program and make it part of your system. I recommend either Peachtree or Quickbooks for businesses that are just starting out.

Lesson 3: Stay on Top of Your Books from Day One

Stay organized, even if that means having an experienced, organized bookkeeper come in once a week to record all the accounting for the business. Staying on top of your numbers will help you analyze the business, help you plan, and help you budget. If you don't do this, you will be running your business in the dark. Who wants that?

Learn the discipline of having a budget in place for your business from day one. Create monthly financials and monitor those financial reports to see how you are doing, reality versus your projections. This discipline will keep you focused on the business and allow you to forecast more and more effectively as time goes on.

Yes, you are busy during the early phases of your business. Yes, this seems like extra work. Yes, it's easy to watch sales come in and think to yourself, "Hey, we must be doing well." But stop right there! If you aren't managing the numbers, if you aren't comparing your forecasts to your reality, you don't know how well you're really doing. Financial information is a management tool, and it gets even more important in the future, when you want to show long-term trends. As Andy was quick to point out to me, I could probably have gotten a significantly better deal when it came time to sell the business to a private equity firm if I'd done a better job early on of setting up my budgets and plans and of measuring the progress against those targets. I would have had good data to pass along!

So, devote a certain amount of time each week to reviewing the numbers. This will help you make good decisions in the short term, use your resources more intelligently as time goes on, and arm you to make important strategic decisions, like what kinds of new customers make the most sense for you to target.

If you still need help on this—and I realize that it's quite possible that you do—consider stopping by the Web site www.GoodAccountants.com, a free service that will put you in front of good candidates and help you find the right person for you.

CHAPTER 16

Why Not You?

*"*Never allow anyone to rain on your parade and thus cast a pall of gloom and defeat on the entire day.*"*

—**Og Mandino, author and sales trainer**

I began this book by urging you to ask yourself this question "Why not me?" I want to close it by reminding you of that all-important question—but this time from two different vantage points we haven't yet explored.

Ask It in Lots of Different Ways

Let's start with the only real "assignment" you're going to get in this chapter: As time goes by, and your business grows, figure out lots of new ways to ask yourself, "Why not me?"

Because I didn't want to distract you, or give you reasons to bail out on the book, I waited until this chapter to tell you—flat out—that you're going to have to find lots of *different* ways to ask yourself "Why not me?" over time. In fact, finding newer and more motivating ways to ask yourself this question is your job description as an entrepreneur. It may well be the most important part of that job description.

You're going to have to come at this question from lots of different angles and use lots of different tools if you want your business to thrive. At the beginning, just thinking about the best answers to this question is likely to be enough. Why shouldn't *you* be the one who turns a dream into a reality? Why shouldn't you be the one who gets to hang out with sports stars or vacation in Hawaii whenever you want? Why shouldn't you be the one who gets to set your working hours?

But as time goes on, you're going to have to give yourself a little more ammunition. You'll know when it's time to up the ante. If simply repeating that question to yourself, and answering it in the usual way isn't enough to help you visualize yourself experiencing the dream, you will need to change course. That's because you're beginning to face a lot of distractions. This, too, is part of your job description—dealing with distractions.

A lot of people are going to try to get you to compromise your vision, or take on their bad day, or sign on with things that don't quite fit your value system, your image of yourself, or your image of your company. And there's going to come a point when those distractions take a toll on you. You're going to have to figure out new ways of visualizing your dream, of running your business.

Og Mandino, the legendary sales trainer and author, once advised: "Remember that no talent, no self-denial, no brains, no character, are required to set up in the fault-finding business. Nothing external can have any power over you unless you permit it. Your time is too precious to be sacrificed in wasted days combating the menial forces of hate, jealousy, and envy. Guard your fragile life carefully. Only God can shape a flower, but any foolish child can pull it to pieces."

REALITY CHECK

The skill set you need to launch a business is not the same as the skill set you need to run a business once it gets to a certain level. At some point you will need to regroup, talk to your mentors, and ask a new set of questions. You will also need to start answering "Why not me?" in a different way.

The distractions are going to escalate and they're going to come at you from different directions. Your business is going to grow and change, you're going to grow and change, and the things that used to motivate you when you were launching the business aren't going to motivate in the same way now. If you don't come up with new answers to the "Why not me?" question, you will give up.

There are going to be days when you hear yourself asking yourself whether it really makes sense to keep going with your business. That's just a fact of life. When you hear that voice, know that it's the sound of not coming up with enough new and updated answers to that "Why not me?" question—answers that match who you are today and where your business is today.

You will need to build new rituals for yourself that engage you in a fresh and innovative way. Only you can say what those rituals should be, but they are probably going to involve some kind of time alone. Initially, your ritual might be going to the gym and working out. Then a few years might go by and you change it to meditating or praying. Then a few more years might go by and you change it again and listen to your favorite music. Just don't get complacent about visualizing the answers to "Why not me?"; if you do, that is the moment you start becoming complacent about your business.

There's a wonderful song that's about entrepreneurship—or it might as well be about entrepreneurship—called "You Get What You Give" by the New Radicals. It's a great "bounceback" song with a great message that has seen millions of people through difficult times since it was released in 1999. There are a lot worse things you could do than to get that song on your iPod and listen to it when you need a pick-me-up.

Keep looking carefully at what's happening to you as a person and keep looking carefully at what's happening to your business as an organization. People are not static things, and neither are businesses. Your business will change regardless of what you set out to do initially. New opportunities will come along and you will need to change on the fly.

For example, when I started my business the Internet was in its infancy and selling a product online was a new thing. My original plan did not call for an Internet strategy. It was a basic bricks-and-mortar model. As time went on, I changed the plan. I knew I could get it done in the way I had laid out originally, but why not take advantage of another way to reach customers? I was not foolish enough to put all my eggs in the "Internet basket," but I did want to make sure we were up and running and had the capability to reach new customers with the new technology.

In short, don't try to master the art of supporting, learning about, and growing your business without also mastering the art of supporting, learning about, and growing *yourself*. Keep track of the lessons you've learned as a person and as a leader, the changes you've made in assessing what's important to you and to those you love, and the best strategies you've figured out for identifying your own best instincts. Those instincts are going to be your real teacher.

The "Why not me?" question is a tool for connecting your business to your heart. Listen to your heart.

Turn It Around

The second vantage point from which to consider the "Why not me?" question has to do with the people you bring into your organization, in any capacity. They could be employees, they could be vendors, they could be customers. Whatever label you put on them, the best of them are going to be important allies for you and your business in the long term. Find ways to help these people ask "Why not me?" about their own dreams.

As an example, let me tell you Sal Parikh's story. I hired Sal as a salesperson years ago. There was a time during his first year when things looked as if they weren't working out with Sal, and I wanted to let him go. My partner Brett talked me out of it because he saw something special in Sal. Brett said,

"Look at him. Every time he gets beat down, he is able to pick himself off the mat and continue to go out there and get back in the fight. He always finds a new reason to start pounding the pavement again. Give him another chance."

It took Sal over two years to really get going, but when he did, the numbers were amazing. His personal resolve was the number-one reason he succeeded. Today he is the top-performing salesperson on a team of over thirty salespeople at our company. Sal succeeded because he never lost faith in himself. He looked around the room and said to himself, "Hey, if these other guys are making deals, why shouldn't I be doing the same thing and getting the same kinds of rewards?" He's having a ball now. That's how it should be.

You can help make these kinds of stories happen in your business. When you do, you are going to feel just great. I can't tell you how satisfying it is to prove to yourself that what goes around really does come around. When you can find a way to take the passion, energy, innocence, competitive spirit, and joy in yourself that you harnessed to get your business off the ground, and you use that to help someone else reach his or her dream, you win the biggest victory of all: getting what you give.

"Many of the most successful men I have known have never grown up. They have retained bubbling-over boyishness. They have relished wit, they have indulged in humor. They have not allowed 'dignity' to depress them into moroseness. Youthfulness of spirit is the twin brother of optimism, and optimism is the stuff of which American business success is fashioned. Resist growing up!**"**

—B. C. Forbes, founder of *Forbes* magazine

Online Resources

Chapter 2

YoungEntrepreneur.com
(www.YoungEntrepreneur.com)
A free online community for young entrepreneurs with over 10,000 members. The site features articles by both members and outside experts, member profile pages and business directory, young entrepreneur success stories, and a very active discussion forum with about 30,000 posts in nearly 5,000 threads. Highly recommended.

Teen Business Link
(www.sba.gov/teens)
A site created by the U.S. Small Business Administration that is targeted at teen entrepreneurs. Good content, but it has a static, low-energy feeling that may turn off some users.

Collegiate Entrepreneurs Association
(www.c-e-o.org/page.php?mode = privateview&pageID = 124)
Doesn't seem to have much of a centralized online community, but there are dozens of local chapters across North America, and many of them have their own Web sites, forums, etc. Worth exploring for the

networking potential if you can identify a local chapter that is right for you.

Young Money

(www.youngmoney.com/entrepreneur/student_entrepreneurs)
Interviews with young celebrities and money experts, tips on managing and growing your money, and much more. Lots of good information here.

Blogs

Odyssey of the Mind

(http://mcmenimon.typepad.com)
Blog site of Travis McMenimon, recent graduate of Villanova University in Villanova, PA, who blogs about "entrepreneurship, business strategy, marketing, branding, IT, and life."

The Entrepreneurial Mind

(http://forum.belmont.edu/cornwall)
Blog site of Dr. Jeff Cornwall, director of the Center for Entrepreneurship at Belmont University, Nashville, TN.

ZeroMillion.com

(www.ryanallis.com/blog)
Blog documenting "the journey of young entrepreneur Ryan Allis as he builds his second company, Broadwick Corporation, to $1 million in sales; publishes his first book, *Zero to One Million*; travels the country as a Web marketing consultant and speaker on young entrepreneurship and personal development; launches his nonprofit organization; and lives the life of a bootstrapping entrepreneur." Ryan is a great example of someone who exemplifies the principles I've discussed in this book.

Young Entrepreneur Journey
(www.successmanifesto.com/blogs/young-entrepreneur)
Blog of the journey of award-winning young entrepreneur and bestselling author Michael Simmons.

The Start-Up Chronicles
(http://bjolin.typepad.com/the_start_up_chronicles)
Blog about The Business // The Journey, an ongoing look into the life of aspiring entrepreneur BJ Olin, president/CEO of Cilantro's Burrito Grill.

Campus Corner: A Young Entrepreneur Returns to College
(www.startupnation.com/blogs)
Fascinating insights from the front lines of both the business and the educational world.

Chapter 3
What Makes a Business Successful

Sade Diya
(http://topten.org/public/AA/AA500.html or
sade@transitiontosuccess.com)
Business and success coach, and CEO of Transition to Success and Founder of Success Builders, an online community of Wealth Builders, who can be visited on the Web. Sade Diya wants you to know: "I can help you create a global presence for your business."

Steve Pavlina
(www.stevepavlina.com/blog/2006/04/10-stupid-mistakes-made-by-the-newly-self-employed)
Blog by a 12-year veteran entrepreneur, who talks about the top ten mistakes that new entrepreneurs make. This will help guide you to

what you should avoid. Also, see www.stevepavlina.com/blog/2007/
01/10-business-lessons-from-a-snarky-entrepreneur.

StartupNation
(www.startupnation.com)
A cool free resource founded by entrepreneurs for entrepreneurs. "We created this site to be your one-stop shop for entrepreneurial success, and we're thrilled that StartupNation has grown to be the leading online content and community resource for entrepreneurs."

How to Stay Motivated

Chris Widener
(www.woopidoo.com/articles/chriswidener/stay-motivated.htm)
A popular American motivational speaker, author, and owner of two very popular motivational Web sites online, he presents an article on how to stay motivated in your work.

EvanCarmichael
(www.evancarmichael.com)
The Internet's #1 resource for small business motivation and strategies. With over 260,000 monthly visitors, 2,100 contributing authors, and 48,000 pages of content, no Web site shares more profiles of famous entrepreneurs and inspires more small business owners than this one.

On Ideas

Bill Doll
(www.billdoll.com/dir/i/i.html)
A blog about billon-dollar ideas. This section focuses on the big ideas, some of which have the potential to change the world. While the general focus is on big business ideas, you will come across noncommercial ideas as well.

Wikipedia
(http://en.wikipedia.org/wiki/List_of_hobbies)
A list of potential hobbies, just to get you started on thinking about what your hobbies might be. A good starting point for brainstorming.

Chapter 4
Setting Goals

How to Set Goals You Will Actually Achieve
(www.stevepavlina.com/blog/2006/08/how-to-set-goals-you-will-actually-achieve)
A great article by Steve Pavlina on the best ways to set goals that you can achieve.

Rules to Setting Business Goals and Objectives
(http://ezinearticles.com/?Rules-to-Setting-Business-Goals-and-Objectives:-Why-and-How-to-be-SMART&id=24276)
Article that will help you make concise goals that make sense and will keep you on track.

Starting in Business Planning
(www.smallbiz.nsw.gov.au/smallbusiness/Starting+in+Business/Business;+Planning)
This site has actual templates that can be used to help you start setting goals.

Short-Term vs. Long-Term Goals

Goal-Setting: Long-Term vs. Short-Term
(http://ezinearticles.com/?Goal-Setting---Long-Term-vs-Short-Term&id=541870)
This Web site can help you differentiate between short- and long-term goals, and discover the importance of both.

Chapter 5
Finding a Business Partner

Leadership Strategies: Your Partner
(www.inc.com/guides/leadership_strat/23041.html)
This article talks about helping people make the right choices when choosing a business partner.

Tips for Finding a Business Partner
(http://startup.partnerup.com/2007/10/26/tips-for-finding-a-business-partner-or-co-founder)
This Web site has tips to think about when searching for your ideal business partner.

Partner Checklist
(www.isquare.com/cklists.cfm#partner)
This Web site offers a checklist of questions to ask yourself about the partner you are going to select.

Good Partner Traits

Eight Essential Characteristics
(http://usmansheikh.wordpress.com/2008/01/09/8-characteristics-of-ideal-business-partners)
This article lists eight ideal characteristics to look for in your future business partner.

Picking a Partner Is Like Picking a Spouse
(www.theglobeandmail.com/servlet/story/
RTGAM.20060616.wwisewords0616/BNSt ory/specialSmallBusiness/
home/?pageRequested=1)
Great article by Sean Wise, mentor to entrepreneurs and start-up companies, via the *Globe and Mail*.

Horror Stories of Business Partners
(www.womenentrepreneur.com/article/1516.html)
Mistakes to avoid in choosing a partner, via womenentrepreneur.com.

Chapter 6
Failure and Success

How Fear of Failure Destroys Success
(www.lifehack.org/articles/lifehack/how-fear-of-failure-destroys-success.htm)
An intriguing article about how the fear of failure can get in the way of achieving success.

Failure
(www.chally.com/enews/failure.html)
An article about how to deal with failure in a positive way and what failure really means, via the Chally organization, a leader in the field of personnel assessment.

Overcome the Fear of Failure
(www.pickthebrain.com/blog/overcome-fear-of-failure)
A blog that offers seven ways to overcome your fears, and shows how fear puts a "cap" on your ability to achieve.

Chapter 7
Priorities in Business

Setting Priorities
(www.allbusiness.com/management/1120170–1.html)
An excellent article that helps you better recognize a priority when it comes to your business, via allbusiness.com.

How to Start Your Own Web Site

How to Start Up a Website
(www.webhostingsearch.com/articles/how-to-start-up-a-website.php)
Some great information on how to start your own Web site. A good starting point.

Web Site Checklist
(www.etproductions.com/help/whats-needed.html)
A checklist of things that should be done before you create your Web site or have someone help you create your site.

4CreatingAWebsite.com
(www.4creatingawebsite.com)
A free step-by-step process for starting a Web site. Worth checking out.

Create Your Own Website
(www.website-builders-review.com/create-your-own-website.php)
Some tips on things to think about when creating the different sections of a Web page.

Some Great Web Site Start-Up Sites

Website Pros
(www.WebsitePros.com)

Network Solutions
(www.NetworkSolutions.com)

Chapter 8

Selling and Promoting

Eight Steps to Success
(www.sitepoint.com/article/business-8-steps-success)
Eight tips to help you sell and promote your business faster.

Cold Calls

Make Cold Calls Work for You
(http://business.blogtells.com/2008/03/17/make-cold-calls-work-for-you-have-fun-on-the-phone)
Helps you find ways to have fun when selling your business over the phone.

Does Cold Calling Work?
(http://recruiter.ducttapemarketing.com/2007/03/does_cold_calli
.html
Why cold calling works and how to be good at it.

Cold Calling
(http://sbinfocanada.about.com/cs/marketing/a/coldcall.htm)
Some helpful tips to think about when making cold calls.

Chapter 9

(www.optimizewebsite.net)
Discusses different aspects of SEO.

(www.seo-web-sites-traffic-optimization.com)
How to increase your Web site traffic.

Chapter 10

Customer Service

Customer Service Zone
(http://customerservicezone.com/customerserviceguest)
Great archive of articles offering advice about what constitutes good customer service.

Customer Service
(www.gaebler.com/Customer-Service.htm)
Tips on how to deliver the most effective customer service, via Gaebler.com.

Money Central's Customer Service Hall of Shame
(http://articles.moneycentral.msn.com/SavingandDebt/Advice/TheCustomerServiceHallOfShame.aspx)
Some customer service horror stories to help you learn what *not* to do.

Making Clients Happy

Five Steps to Making Your Customer Happy
(http://ezinearticles.com/?5-Steps-To-Making-Your-Customer-Happy&id=191279)
A summary of simple and effective tips.

Making Angry Customers Happy Customers
(http://particletree.com/notebook/making-angry-customers-happy-customers)
It's easier than you may think, as this site proves.

Customer–Client Communications

Communicating with Clients
(www.akamarketing.com/communicating-with-clients.html)
A good summary of basic strategies.

Chapter 12

Hiring

Service Corps of Retired Executives
(www.score.org/60_guide_employee-recruiting.html)
Hiring good people can be hard; check out this article on what it
takes to hire and keep valuable employees.

Fast Company on Hiring by Attitude
(www.fastcompany.com/magazine/04/hiring.html)
How to hire people for their attitude and then train them to master
the right skill.

Vault.com on Effective Hiring
(www.vault.com/nr/newsmain.jsp?nr_page = 3&ch_id = 400&
article_id = 3093002&cat_id = 1261)
Want to know how to hire better people faster? Check out this article.

Findlaw.com on Hiring
(http://smallbusiness.findlaw.com/employment-employer/employment
-employer-hiring)
Information about the hiring process, from the initial advertisement
for a position to the signing of a contract.

Chapters 12 and 13

Effective Salespeople

NFIB on the Sales Team
(www.nfib.com/object/1583720.html)
A good article on what makes a sales staff effective.

Running the Meeting
(www.allbusiness.com/sales/1011–1.html)
Are you nervous about conducting your first business meeting? Check out this advice from allbusiness.com for help on how to conduct an effective business meeting.

Credibility

Establishing Credibility
(www.grokdotcom.com/establishingcredibility.htm)
Some pointers on how to establish credibility with potential clients.

Saleslobby
(www.saleslobby.com/Mag/1202/FEKT.asp)
Seven helpful steps in establishing credibility with top executives.

Chapters 14 and 15

Lawyers/Accountants

Five Questions to Ask
(www.microsoft.com/smallbusiness/resources/finance/legal-expenses/
hiring-a-lawyer-5-questions-to-ask.aspx#Hiringalawyerquestionsto
ask)
The right questions to ask when hiring a lawyer, via Microsoft's small business library.

How to Hire a Lawyer
(http://consumerlawpage.com/article/howhire.shtml)
Mistakes to avoid when hiring a lawyer, via ConsumerLawPage.com.

Hiring a Lawyer
(www.centernetworks.com/hiring-a-lawyer)
A blog about entrepreneurs and their lawyers, and why it is important
to have one.

The Right Accountant
(www.entrepreneur.com/money/moneymanagement/bookkeeping/
article45628.html)
A good discussion of the importance of finding the right accountant,
via Entrepreneur.com.

Seven Questions
(www.nfib.com/object/3655353.html)
Seven important questions to ask yourself about the accountant you
are going to hire.

GoodAccountants.com
(www.GoodAccountants.com)
A free service that will put you in front of good candidates and help
you find the right person for you.

Chapter 16

BusinessWeek **magazine (archives)**
(www.businessweek.com/magazine/content/06_28/b3992001.htm)
Some good articles on how failure can lead to success, as well as some
important lessons on how to learn from your (apparent) failures.